SWIMMING/DIVING

A total guide to super swimming and diving!

Charles Carson, Jr.

A *Sports Illustrated For Kids* Book

First Edition

Library of Congress Cataloging-in-Publication Data

Carson, Charles.
    Make the team : swimming and diving / Charles Carson. — 1st ed.
        p.   cm.
    "A Sports illustrated for kids book."
    Summary: Describes the basic skills, common strokes and dives, and training exercises involved in competitive swimming and diving.
    ISBN 0-316-13027-3.
    ISBN 0-316-13028-1 (pb)
    1. Swimming—Juvenile literature.   2. Diving—Juvenile literature.
[1. Swimming.   2. Diving.]   I. Title.
GV837.6.C37 1991
797.2'1—dc20   90-46569

SPORTS ILLUSTRATED FOR KIDS is a trademark of
THE TIME INC. MAGAZINE COMPANY.

Sports Illustrated For Kids Books is a joint imprint of Little, Brown and Company and Warner Juvenile Books. This title is published in arrangement with Cloverdale Press Inc.

10 9 8 7 6 5 4 3 2 1

BP

For further information regarding this title, write to Little Brown and Company, 34 Beacon Street, Boston, MA 02108

Published simultaneously in Canada by Little, Brown & Company (Canada) Limited

Printed in the United States of America

Interior design by Bernard Springsteel
Interior illustrations by Stanford Kay/Paragraphics

Dedication

For Vicki Davies, Ray Bussard, and my parents.

Acknowledgments

Janet L. Gabriel, Director of Education, Safety and Development, United States Diving

Rose Milo, Director of Age Group Programs, United States Swimming

Ray Bussard, University of Tennessee Men's Swimming Coach (retired); 1984 U.S. Olympic Swimming Coach

John Trembley, University of Tennessee Men's Swimming Coach; Director, United Swimming Clinics

Vince Panzano, Ohio State University Diving Coach

The Chattanooga News-Free Press

Jacqueline Carson, Kent Ferguson, Jeff Gordon, Bruce Hayes, Betsy Mitchell, Jay Mortenson, Rick Reynolds, Jim Whalen, John Witchel

CONTENTS

INTRODUCTION

Swimmers: Ride high. Divers: Ride, hang and rip. Ride high? Rip? What do these words mean? These are terms used by swimmers and divers. If you like to swim, this book can teach you about "riding high" in the water. If you like to dive, you can learn about "riding the board," "hang time" in the air, and "ripping" your entries.

Swimming and diving are very different sports, and each has its own training methods and muscle requirements. Swimmers perform in the water and race their opponents up the length of a pool. Whoever is fastest, wins, just like in a running race at a track meet. A diver per-

For many, the freestyle stroke or front crawl is the easiest to learn.

forms in the air. Each dive is scored by judges, and the diver with the highest score wins, like in gymnastics.

About the only thing the two sports have in common is water. Both sports take place at a swimming pool, and meets feature competition in both swimming and diving. Diving is normally held during breaks in a swimming meet, to give swimmers a chance to rest. Having both sports in a single meet also helps draw a larger crowd.

Today, swimming and diving competitions offer opportunities for young people. Swimming and diving meets are probably held in almost every city and town. If you have the talent and practice hard enough, you may even earn a spot on a national team and travel to other countries to compete.

Many kids start competing on neighborhood teams in the summer. These are age group programs, and kids compete against other kids in their same age range.

You may even be able to compete for a school team, though probably not until you reach junior or senior high. Many high school swimmers and divers also belong to a YMCA, YWCA or community team. In these programs, you can qualify for regional and national championship meets, such as the Y invitational meets or the Junior Olympics.

You can continue to compete in college, and even after college in programs called masters swimming and diving. So you can see that these sports offer you a chance to maintain skills for a lifetime of fitness and competition.

At about age 10 or 11, most kids decide on their favorite sport and whether to train for that sport year round. A lot of swimmers and divers also like other sports like tennis, gymnastics, basketball, baseball or football. Deciding what sport to concentrate on depends on your natural ability, as well as on which sports you love the most. Most college swimmers and divers have been training five days a week every week for several years, but they continue to play other sports for recreation and variety.

Maybe this will help you decide: Swimming is one of the best exercises for your heart, lungs and overall body conditioning. Like many competitive swimmers, you may find you simply like the feeling of working out in water.

Swimming and diving teach self-discipline, control and confidence, and they teach you how to be a good loser and

A back dive in a layout position makes this diver look as if he's flying!

a gracious winner. Most of all, you will develop pride in your personal achievement. When you're in the middle of the dive or race, it's your effort alone that helps you finish. It's a great feeling to know you've given it your all.

Learning the athletic and safety skills required in swimming and diving will also open you up to other aquatic sports—water polo, synchronized swimming, skin diving, snorkeling, water skiing, surfing, canoeing and sailing. And every one of these is a lot of fun.

This book is geared to help those just starting competitive swimming and diving. But even if you have been competing for a while, you will find new things in this book to think about and practice.

Whether you choose swimming or diving as your main interest, you can learn a lot by reading about the other sport too. Understanding the concept of skill progressions in the diving section can be of benefit to swimmers. And the swimming section on goal setting and how the body adapts to training can be very helpful to divers.

One thing is certain: To make the team in swimming or diving, you'll have to practice. Listen to the voice of experience—Dave Berkoff, who won a gold medal at the 1988 Olympics and also holds the world record for the 100-meter backstroke. "I never thought I'd be a top swimmer," says Dave. "I worked since I was six years old swimming. It was a very, very slow, gradual progression. After a lot of work and a lot of training, it came to me."

If you've already mastered basic water skills and now want to learn more about training and competition, the information is here. The first time you stand on that springboard or starting block could be the start of something really big.

Chapter 1

SWIMMING— TAKING THE PLUNGE

Some Swimming History

People have been swimming for thousands of years. Paintings that date from about 9000 B.C. on the rock walls of caves in Libya show people swimming. Children of kings and noble families in Egypt were taught to swim as early as 2100 B.C. Young boys in ancient Greece and Rome learned to swim as part of their schooling.

Historians believe the earliest swim races in Japan took place in 36 B.C. At about the same time, the first heated pool was built in Rome.

During the Middle Ages of Europe, knights and soldiers sometimes learned to swim, but a lot of people thought swimming helped spread disease. This is not true, of course. Later, in the 1400s, swimming for recreation and medical therapy became more common. *The Art of Swimming*, one of the first known books on the sport, was published in Europe in 1538. There is mention of swimming among the Incas in South America in 1448, and in Colombia in 1536. The Japanese made it compulsory in schools in 1603. In the late 1700s, shortly after the United States gained independence, Benjamin Franklin became the first famous North American to write about how much he enjoyed swimming.

Swimming developed for both recreation and sport in English-speaking countries during the 1800s. In 1837, there were six indoor pools in London, England. Most people swam using a form of breaststroke or sidestroke, keeping both arms under the water at all times.

A stroke called the "trudgen" was demonstrated by John Trudgen in London in 1873. It was the first swim-

Many recreational swimmers use the breaststroke as a rest stroke. But competitive breaststrokers go quite fast.

ming style in which both arms came out of the water before going forward to pull again, and was similar to the front crawl.

Hawaiians and Solomon Islanders swam a version of the crawl stroke, today called freestyle, in the late 1800s. Henry Wickham of Australia began using the crawl in 1893.

The backstroke developed in the early 1900s. At first, backstrokers used an upside-down breaststroke kick, and their arms stayed underwater and pulled down from the sides. As swimmers began using the overhead stroke, pulling their arms out of the water after each stroke, they switched from the breaststroke kick to the flutter kick.

Butterfly became an official competitive stroke in 1953, although swimmers had been using a form of the butterfly during breaststroke races for 20 years. American swimmer Henry Myers used the breaststroke kick, but his arms came out of the water between each stroke to recover and begin the next stroke. Traditional breaststrokers keep their arms under water during the stroke and the recovery. The rules did not separate the strokes until swimmers began using the dolphin kick together with the over-water recovery, producing a much more

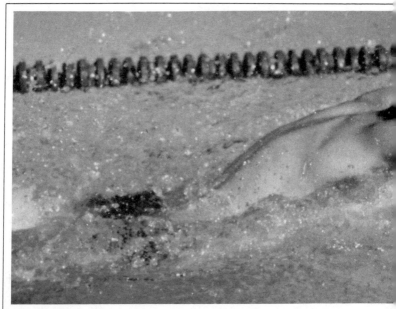

The butterfly stroke is the most powerful competitive stroke—

powerful and faster stroke than the breaststroke. Today, competitive swimming is made up of the breaststroke, butterfly, backstroke and freestyle strokes.

Swimming was not a part of the ancient Olympics, but three outdoor races were held for men at the first modern Olympics in Athens, Greece, in 1896. The winners were from Hungary and Austria. Swimmers said the water was freezing. Women's races were added in the Stockholm Olympics in 1912, and the first female winners were from Australia and Great Britain.

Americans have done well in Olympic swimming events from the beginning. Charles Daniels won America's first gold medals in the 200- and 440-yard freestyle

and awesome to look at.

races in St. Louis in 1904. Duke Paoa Kahanamoku, a popular Hawaiian, won the 100-meter freestyle in 1912 and 1920, and finished second in 1924 at age 33.

Television announcer Donna de Varona was the youngest member of the U.S. Olympic Swimming Team at Rome in 1960. She was 13. She made the U.S. Olympic Team again for the 1964 Tokyo Olympics. This time she won two gold medals. Also in 1964, Don Schollander became the first swimmer to win four gold medals in a single Olympics. Two of his wins were in individual events, and two were with his American teammates on relays. Debbie Meyer was the first swimmer to win three gold medals in individual events in one Olympics, at Mexico City in 1968. Mark Spitz did even better at Munich in 1972, winning an amazing seven gold medals in four individual events and three relays. Recent American Olympic champions include Janet Evans, Matt Biondi, Tracy Caulkins, Mary T. Meagher and Steve Lundquist.

Swimming Today

American success in international swimming is a direct result of the age group swimming programs in cities and towns all over the country. Summer camps have taught kids to swim for many years, but summer recreational swimming leagues really took off after World War II when pools were built in many growing suburbs.

Summer swim leagues and other age group programs offer competition for girls and boys in the following age divisions: 8-and-under, 9-10, 11-12, 13-14 and 15-16. These categories give you a chance to swim against other kids your own age. There are now so many kids participating that U.S. Swimming (U.S.S.) keeps national rankings for each age group in every stroke and distance.

U.S.S. is age group swimming's national organization. It makes sure age group swimming meets are organized in a standard way. It sets guidelines for small swim meets, such as between two neighborhood country club teams, and for big meets, such as the national championships which select swimmers to represent the USA in meets overseas.

U.S. Swimming is a member of FINA (*fee*-nah). In French, FINA stands for *Federation Internationale de Natation Amateur.* The English translation is, the International Federation of Amateur Aquatics. FINA was founded in 1908 to draw up rules for swimming, diving and water polo events all over the world. Synchronized swimming later became a part of FINA.

FINA maintains world record lists and is responsible for organizing aquatics at the Olympic Games. FINA also holds world championship meets each year preceding the summer Olympics.

In the U.S., there are two swimming seasons each year, a short-course season and a long-course season. In the short-course season, swimmers compete in a pool that's 25 yards or 25 meters long. Most YMCA, YWCA, high school and college pools in the U.S. are 25 yards long. The short-course season takes part during the school year, from August or September through February or March. In the rest of the world, most short-course meets are swum in 25-meter pools.

During the short-course season, swimmers may compete in meets that have different sets of rules to follow. The National Interscholastic Swimming Coaches Association (NISCA) governs meets between school teams, and

NISCA has its own set of rules. The YMCA and YWCA have also established their own rules.

The long-course season runs from April or May to August. Long-course pools are 50 meters long. This is the length of the pools used for the Olympics, world championships and most international events. World records can be set only in 50-meter pools. U.S. Swimming, however, does keep records of the best times swum in 25-yard pools. These are American or U.S. Open short-course records.

Olympic swimming gets lots of national and international publicity. But for many years, some of the fastest swimming in the world has taken place at U.S. colleges and universities. In fact, many swimmers from other countries study and train in the U.S. because of the excellent college swimming programs.

College swimming in the U.S. is governed by the National Collegiate Athletic Association (NCAA). Most NCAA rules are similar to FINA's.

Schools in NCAA swimming are grouped into three divisions. In general, large schools are members of Division I. Michigan, Yale, Indiana, USC, Texas and Stanford have all won the men's Division I title more than once. Texas, Florida and Stanford have strong women's Division I swimming teams. Smaller schools, such as Kenyon College in Ohio, also have excellent programs. Kenyon has won Division III titles for both men and women.

Younger swimmers up to age 18 can compete at regional and national Junior Olympics meets. Swimming is also a part of the U.S. Olympic Festival, a multi-sport competition sponsored by the U.S. Olympic Committee and held in each non-Olympic year. The Olympic Festival gives Olympic hopefuls a chance to gain experience in a meet set up just like the Olympics. Other big swimming meets include the World Championships, Pan American Games, the Pan Pacifics, and the World University Games. You can see many of these meets on TV, and you can learn a lot by watching the champions swim.

Now it's time to learn about Riding High.

Ride High

Ride High means to swim as high in the water as possible. Bodies move faster in air than in water. The more of your body that you can get "up and out" of the water, the faster you will go. The key to riding high is to keep your shoulders out of the water without letting your legs sink, which creates drag.

Drag is the resistance of the water, and it is what slows you down. When you swim, all of your effort is spent trying to overcome drag. To swim faster, you need to reduce drag as much as possible.

A pool full of waves is turbulent and has more resistance than a pool full of still water. Of course it is the swimmers who cause these waves when they swim. You can't do much about the waves created by other swimmers, but you can reduce the amount of turbulence you create around yourself by streamlining.

Streamlining means stretching out your body into a position that's as smooth and straight as possible. A body that moves too much from side to side, or up and down, slows down a swimmer's forward motion more than a body that is streamlined. Keep your lower body in line with your shoulders without wiggling your hips from side to side. Also, armstrokes that are short and choppy create

A good racing dive is essential to winning in competitive swimming.

a lot of turbulence in front of you. Long, streamlined arm-strokes will keep the turbulence and drag to a minimum.

In fact, streamlining reduces drag during all parts of a race. That includes streamlining in the air when you push off the block for a racing start, and streamlining on your underwater push off the wall after doing a turn.

Bubbles that cling to your body also create drag. Swim slowly and watch your arms underwater. You'll see that

little bubbles stick to the skin of your hands and arms. Some of this bubble drag can be reduced by improving the entry of your hands and arms on each armstroke. Bubbles also get caught in body hair. That's why older swimmers at championship meets "shave down." By shaving the hair off their arms, legs and bodies, they remove places for bubbles to stick, and this reduces drag.

We'll look at the four competitive swimming strokes

in a moment, and talk about how you can ride high in each to reduce drag. But first, let's look at the equipment used in competitive swimming.

Equipment

One of the nice things about swimming is that you don't have to buy balls, gloves or a lot of other equipment. Most of the equipment you use will be the property of the team, and stored at the pool. Team dues may help pay for that equipment.

Swimsuit

Obviously, you need a swimsuit. Most training suits are made of nylon or lycra. Suits for girls are more expensive because more fabric is used to cover the body.

Choose a suit that fits snugly but doesn't pinch around your legs. Girls may want to try on several different designs to find a suit with straps that are comfortable at the shoulders. Chemicals in the pool damage the elastic in suits after awhile, so you should have one or two swimsuits for training, and a separate suit in your team's color for competition. That suit may be cut higher in the legs, and for girls, it may have less material covering the back. Here's a speed tip: Keep the racing suit fresh by rinsing it out in cold water after every use. Otherwise it will quickly get baggy and cause drag by trapping water.

Some swimmers wear two suits at the same time when they are training to cause more drag. The suit worn on top is called the *drag suit* because it helps trap air and water against your body. When you get used to going fast wearing two suits, racing in one will make you faster.

Goggles

Chemicals in swimming pool water can irritate your eyes, so it's important to wear goggles. Goggles come in all different shapes, sizes and colors—some even have mirror surfaces. A good pair for both training and racing costs only a few dollars. Fancy extras such as anti-fog lenses or neon frames can add to the cost.

Most sporting goods stores have samples you can try on. Make sure that the nose band is comfortable, and that the lenses are far enough from your eyes so that your eyelashes don't rub against them.

Also make sure that the goggles form a watertight seal around your eyes. Press the lenses against your face so that they feel snug but not uncomfortable. If they're tight enough, you will be able to do all four strokes and flip turns without water leaking in.

Kickboards and Pull Buoys

Kickboards are usually made of flat pieces of styrofoam. They let you keep your head out of the water and your upper body riding high while you propel yourself forward using just your legs. Most swimmers put their hands on the kickboard somewhere between the front edge and the middle. Whatever hand position is most comfortable for you, keep your arms straight and relaxed without laying your chest on the board.

A pull buoy is usually made of two round pieces of styrofoam tied together. You hold the pull buoy between your legs at the top of your thighs. It helps keep your legs high in the water and prevents you from kicking. Swimming with a pull buoy isolates your arms and helps you develop upper body strength. The stronger you are in your upper body, the easier it will be to ride high in the water as you swim.

Paddles, Gloves and Fins

Some swimmers use plastic hand paddles to help them pull and push through the water. Paddles develop strength in your lower arms and shoulders, and they help you learn to reach farther to increase your "distance per stroke." Not all swimming programs use paddles because sometimes they can cause shoulder problems. Webbed gloves work much the same way. Your coach can help you determine if you should use paddles or gloves in your workouts.

Rubber fins are the flippers that scuba divers wear on their feet to propel themselves underwater. Competitive swimmers sometimes train with flippers to learn to keep their legs relaxed, and to increase the flexibility of their ankles. Flippers are also great when you are learning the dolphin (or butterfly) kick.

Beginning Skills

Let's assume you already know basic swimming skills and can tread water and dive to retrieve objects off the pool bottom. Here are some more training tips to help you get started swimming competitively.

Hands and Feet

Hold your hands with your fingers spread slightly apart. The wrist will bend a bit forward or backward, depending on which stroke you're swimming.

Some coaches will tell you to use your hands like paddles. This does not mean you should hold your fingers tight together and your wrists rigid and straight. Instead, you should relax your hands. Keep your thumb separated from your fingers, and think about grabbing water in front of you and pulling yourself through it.

Your feet should also be relaxed, and your ankles should be flexible. Most swim kicks actually begin high up in the leg, in the hips and thighs. The only time you curl your toes up towards the knee is during one part of the breaststroke kick. The feet normally add the final "flip" or "flick" at the end of the kick. So when it comes to your feet, think *flick,* not *kick.*

Breathing

Many animals that live in the water, like tadpoles and fish, never have to come to the surface to breathe. They get all the oxygen they need from the water through their gills. People are mammals, like dolphins, whales and seals, and we have to come to the surface to get our oxygen from the air. Every Olympic swimmer once had to learn the same basic breathing skills that you need now.

The hardest part about breathing while you swim is learning not to hold your breath when your face is in the water. Holding your breath is a natural reaction. But think about how you breathe normally. You continuously inhale-exhale, inhale-exhale. When you swim, you should also inhale and exhale continuously.

Did your first swim teacher tell you to put your face in the water and "make bubbles like a motor boat?" It's silly, but it works! You learn to blow air out of your lungs in the water that way. You'd be surprised how many people forget that skill when they're swimming.

Some swimmers exhale from their mouths, some from their noses, and some from both their mouth and nose. During a freestyle flip turn, swimmers exhale almost entirely from their noses, which keeps the water out. When you take a breath, turn your head and "inhale" through your mouth. Remember, don't hold your breath at all. As soon as your face goes back in the water, begin blowing out the air. Exhale continuously until you are ready to take your next breath, and be sure to exhale completely. Blow *all* the way out, and really empty your lungs.

A good way to practice this is to bob up and down in the deep end of a pool, where the water is a foot or two above your head. Tread water a little way from the side, rise up, take a breath and then blow it out as you sink feet first to the bottom. Continue blowing out as you touch and push off the bottom. Get a rhythm going, where you

Kickboards help swimmers concentrate on their leg movement during practice sessions.

finish blowing all your air out just before you bob to the surface again for the inhale. Try bobbing this way 20 times to practice the continuous inhale-exhale, inhale-exhale that you'll need for a top performance.

Breathing the wrong way—for instance, holding your breath—wastes energy that you need to ride high in the water. Some swimmers have a beautiful freestyle stroke but they lift their heads too high or jerk their heads to the side when they turn to breathe. These problems can cause your legs to drop, which creates more drag and slows you down!

Practice your breathing. When you get good at it, you'll be a better swimmer.

The Four Competitive Strokes

The normal order of learning the strokes is pretty much the same as their order of difficulty. First, you learn freestyle and then comes backstroke, breaststroke and butterfly. You will probably spend your first year on a swim team learning the correct technique for each stroke. By the end of your second full year, you should be able to do all four strokes fairly well.

Freestyle or Crawl Stroke

This is the fastest stroke and the easiest to learn. As you stroke with your arms, your legs *flutter kick,* each moving up and down, one at a time.

Freestyle Kick or Flutter Kick

The flutter kick can be done with two beats, four beats or six beats for every armstroke (a "beat" is one kick by one leg). In general, sprinters use a six-beat kick, and dis-

1. Your right hand enters the water directly in front of your shoulder, with your thumb angled toward the bottom of the pool. Your hand pulls down and slightly to the outside. This is the *catch.* Your legs are busy flutter kicking. Your left arm has finished its pull and your hand is at your side.

2. Your right hand pulls under your chest while your left hand reaches ahead and enters the water in front of the right shoulder. Don't forget to exhale completely.

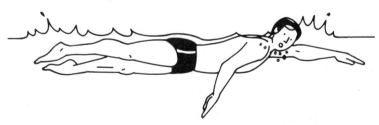

3. Your right hand pushes toward your leg and your head turns to the right side to breathe. Your left hand starts to pull through the water.

4. Inhale as the arm leaves the water behind you. Turn your head so your face returns to the water as you reach forward with your right arm. At this point, your left arm will have started its pull.

tance freestylers use a two-beat kick. Your coach can help you figure out which will be best for you.

Again, relax your feet and ankles. Think of kicking from the hips and not the knees. Kicking from the knee is the most common mistake of beginners. Making a big splash is not effective or fast. It makes your legs tired, and that means your arms must work harder to pull you through the water.

You can use a kickboard to practice the flutter kick, or you can kick on your side. To kick on your right side, put your right arm straight over your head and hold your left arm down at your side. Kick six beats and then turn your head to breathe. Turn your head back under and continue kicking and breathing every six kicks for one length of the pool. Come back kicking on your left side.

Freestyle Pull

When you pull your arm through the water, keep your elbow up. The lower part of your arm, from the elbow to the hand, does the actual pulling. If you drop your elbow, the lower arm can't grab as much water.

Some swimmers keep their arms straight when they bring them out of the water to recover from the end of one stroke to the beginning of the next. For most people, the best way to recover is to bend the arm and keep the elbow high. A good way to practice relaxing your arm on the recovery is to think of dragging your fingertips along the surface of the water next to your body.

Other freestyle pulling drills include swimming with one arm for a length of the pool. Keep the arm you're not using stretched out in front of you, and breathe every four strokes. Swim one length with one arm and another length with the other arm. You can also use pull buoys to help you learn to breathe on both sides. Breathing on both sides increases your endurance and balance by making sure both arms are equally strong.

The "catch-up drill" is a pulling drill that helps you learn "body roll." The best freestylers roll a bit from side to side with each armstroke. They do this by rotating their shoulders, not the head.

To do the catch-up drill, start with both arms in front of you. Pull one full stroke with your left arm. As you begin the pull, "roll" your left side toward the pool bottom as you feel your right arm extend farther in front of you. Keep the right arm out front as you finish your stroke with your left arm. Roll your body back to a level position as the left hand extends to "catch up" to the right hand. Then, begin a right armstroke. Roll your right side toward the pool bottom as you stretch your left arm farther in front of you. Level off again as your right hand "catches up" to the left hand. Do this for two lengths of the pool, breathing every four strokes on either your right or left side.

Body roll helps you extend your arms as far as possible

to get the most out of each pull. If you roll too much, you'll create drag instead.

A still head position is very important. Keep your head up so that you can look forward instead of straight down at the pool bottom. It's easier to ride high if the line of the water's surface goes right across your eyebrows.

Freestyle Flip Turn

Beginners use *open turns* at the wall at the end of a lap. To do an open turn, you grab the wall, lift your head out of the water, pull your legs to the wall and then push off again. Competitive swimmers use *flip turns* because they are faster. They are also easy to learn.

Start by doing somersaults in the water away from the wall. As you do each one, blow air out of your nose so water doesn't get in. Tuck your chin, roll forward, and use your arms to pull yourself all the way around. Keep your arms stretched straight over your head as you come back up to a standing position.

Now try doing the somersault close to the wall. If your pool has a "T" painted on the bottom to mark the lane, stand at the top of the "T." Tumble, and stretch your arms over your head after you pull yourself around. As you somersault, twist onto your side. As your feet re-enter the water, stretch them toward the wall to push off. As soon as your feet touch, push off on your side rather than your stomach. Think "Flip. Twist. Push."

Practice to see how close you need to be so that after you flip, your feet reach the wall with your legs bent, as if you were going to jump. Soon, you'll learn to adjust how much you need to extend or bend your legs. Finally, practice the turn by swimming into the wall, starting about

1. When you approach the wall, start your flip turn by dropping your head and tucking your chin against your chest.

2. As you pull down with your arms, your body will follow your head into a somersault.

3. Bring your knees to your chest as you come around. When your arms have finished their pull, they start stretching out over your head.

4. Straighten your legs to bring your feet against the side of the pool. Your arms are now over your head. Start turning your body clockwise or counterclockwise to return to the freestyle position.

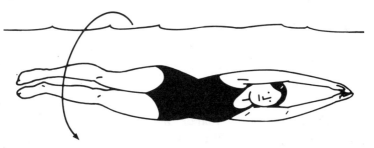

5. Push off from the end of the pool with your legs and feet while your body finishes turning. You are now back in the freestyle position. Point your arms toward the surface so you can glide back on top of the water and start your next stroke.

four strokes away. Work back farther until you do a whole lap before the flip.

Backstroke

Backstroke is like doing freestyle on your back, with a few important differences. You stroke with one arm at a time and use an underwater "S"-shaped pull. Flutter kick with your legs. Most backstrokers use a six-beat kick.

Since you're on your back, your face is out of the water. That makes breathing simple, but you can't see where you're going! Backstrokers learn to count how many strokes it takes to swim a lap so they always know how far they are from the wall. At an indoor pool, you can also use ceiling markings and lights as a guide. During races, backstroke flags are placed about five meters from the end of the pool so you can tell how much farther you have to go to finish your lap.

Backstroke breathing? Inhale on one arm pull and exhale on the other. It's that simple. But again, be sure you blow out all of your air before taking another breath. Some backstrokers whose arms turn over more slowly may inhale and exhale on every stroke.

Backstroke Pull

Be careful not to put your arms in the water too wide. Pretend your body is a clock, with your head at 12 o'clock and your feet at 6. Practice placing your hands in the water at 11 and 1 o'clock.

A good backstroke pulling drill is to swim with one arm for each lap, like the one-arm freestyle drill. The arm not in use is kept by your side instead of out front. The most important part of this stroke is the "finish." Push your hand hard toward the bottom of the pool when it's by your thigh, before you bring your arm back out of the water. That last extra push will give you the racer's edge in speed!

"Kids starting out often turn their arms over too fast, and don't push through enough at the end of the stroke," says Olympic swimmer Dave Berkoff. He should know— he holds the world record for the 100-meter backstroke. "The final push is the most powerful part of the armstroke.

That's the part you want to accelerate hard and fast."

Practice body roll when you backstroke too. As you pull with your left arm, your left side will tilt toward the bottom. Keep your head still and lift your right shoulder out of the water. Reverse it when you are pulling with your right arm.

Backstroke Turns

Beginners often use open turns with backstroke just like they do with freestyle. Eventually you will want to know how to do the backstroke flip turn, because it's faster.

Learning the basic backstroke flip turn is a bit different from learning the freestyle flip turn. You don't really do a full somersault. It's more of a "pivot" than a "flip."

Practice by floating on your back one arm-length away from the wall. Place one hand flat on the wall, with your fingers pointing down. Your hand should be about six inches to a foot below the water surface. Push against the wall with your hand. Bend your legs at the knees and keep your feet together. Pull your knees toward your chest and swing your legs around toward the arm touching the wall as you push away from the wall with your hand.

Place your feet against the wall. Your arms should be stretched overhead in the direction opposite the wall. Push off with your feet as soon as they touch, keeping your body streamlined. Stay underwater for several yards or meters rather than bob right back to the surface.

As soon as you push off, start flutter kicking even before you start stroking with your arms.

Backstroke Kick

Champion backstrokers are usually good kickers. The

kick isn't deep, though. Try to keep your toes as close to the surface as possible. Think of flicking the surface with your toes. Keep your hips high and stay flat on top of the water – ride high. Tuck your chin so you can almost see your feet, but keep your chin off your chest. Practice your flutter kick by kicking on your back, clasping both hands straight overhead, breathing continuously.

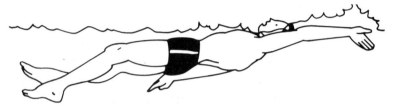

1. Your left arm enters the water directly over your shoulder. Turn your hand so it enters the water, little finger first, with your thumb pointing toward the ceiling. Flutter kick rapidly with a six-beat kick.

2. Your left elbow bends as you sweep your hand back toward your body. Your right arm begins to recover out of the water. Think about keeping your right shoulder out of the water. You'll need to roll your body to do this.

3. Your right arm has come over your head while the left arm has begun to push back toward your feet. The legs continue flutter kicking.

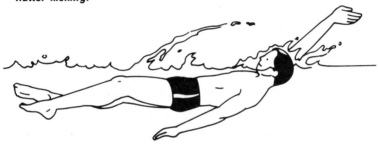

4. When your left hand is near your thigh, push it strongly down toward the bottom of the pool. Meanwhile, your right hand enters the water, little finger first. Then lift your left hand sideways out of the water.

Breaststroke

Breaststroke is the only stroke where your arms recover under the water. Lifesaving classes teach the breaststroke for energy conservation. When you swim it slowly, you can do the breaststroke for a long time. In competition, however, it can be very tiring, because your legs are an important part of the breaststroke's forward movement.

The leg muscles are larger than the other muscles in your body. It takes a lot of energy to keep your leg muscles going, and swimming fast uses a lot of energy.

Breathing while you're swimming the breaststroke is pretty simple: Breathe once for every armstroke.

Coordinating the movement of your arms and legs is the hardest part of the breaststroke. Fast breaststrokers have very different styles—some lift their entire chests high out of the water, and some stay close to the surface. It's an individual thing your coach can help you work on. Most of all, watch other swimmers. Practice, practice, practice, and you'll get it.

Breaststroke Pulling and Kicking

You can use a pull buoy to practice breaststroke, but it tends to make the arm motion smaller. You have to really work to be sure you extend your arms fully in front of you. Think of lifting your shoulders up and forward as you breathe. Also, after you catch the water, don't pull your hands apart much wider than your shoulders.

Practicing the breaststroke kick holding a kickboard helps increase your ankle strength and flexibility. The kickboard makes it easier to feel your feet pushing the water back. Here's a drill to try without a kickboard: Hold

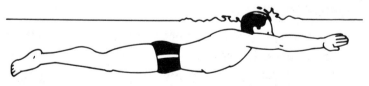

1. Start with your arms in front of you, with your thumbs tilted down to the bottom of the pool. The beginning part of the pull is the catch.

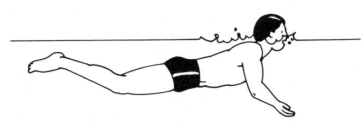

2. Keeping your elbows up, pull the lower part of both arms out and down. Feel the water pushing against your lower arms. Start lifting your head to inhale. Pull your hands back and in toward your chest. Bend your legs at the knees.

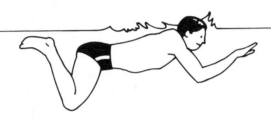

3. Put your face back in the water and exhale. Bring your heels up toward your buttocks. Begin thrusting your hands forward, turning your hands so your thumbs point down.

4. Kick by whipping your feet out, around, and back together as you extend your arms forward, ready to begin your next stroke.

your hands at your sides and try to touch your fingertips with your calves before you whip your feet around and straighten your legs. This isn't easy—you have to really work to lift your head to breathe every two or three kicks—but it sure will make you stronger.

Breaststroke Turn and Underwater Pulldown

There are no flips involved during a breaststroke turn. Swim to the wall and keep both shoulders level as you touch with both hands at the same time. Be sure you touch the wall—don't grab the gutter. Remove one hand as quickly as possible as you bend your knees, pull your feet up under you and press your feet against the wall. Push off underwater, twisting sideways, which is faster than rotating all the way to your stomach.

In competition breaststroke, you're allowed one full underwater arm pull and kick after you do a turn before you must come back to the surface. The underwater arm-stroke is called a *pulldown*. You must be flat on your stomach when you start the pulldown.

Concentrate on streamlining. Keep your head in line with your body. Don't tuck in your chin too much or lift your head to watch where you're going. Stretch your arms straight out over your head. You'll feel yourself starting to slow down after the push off the wall. That's when you do your underwater armstroke. Your head must break the surface, which gives you a chance to breathe. Then start swimming the whole stroke again.

Butterfly

Butterfly is usually the last stroke learned for two reasons. First, it's difficult to coordinate the timing of the kick and the pull. Second, butterfly tires you out more quickly than the other strokes. You will need to build a certain amount of endurance to be able to practice butterfly for more than a lap or two at a time. Maintaining proper form takes even more out of you. But butterfly is the fastest stroke after freestyle. Once you learn to swim butterfly, it may become your favorite stroke.

Butterfly or Dolphin Kick

There are two kicks for every armstroke in the butterfly, but many beginners make the mistake of trying to make the kicks equal in "splash." That's usually what throws the timing off and prevents swimmers from learning the right "dolphin" action.

Each kick is actually about the same in strength, but the kick that comes right before you breathe usually looks bigger because it makes a more noticeable splash and sound (diagram 4, page 47).

Try to think of moving forward, rather than up and down, as you do the butterfly. Work on getting your shoulders out of the water and swing your arms around, not up. That will help you keep your hips on the surface and make it easier to ride high. Remember to kick from the hips and thighs and not from the knees.

You can practice the dolphin kick using a kickboard, or by kicking on your side the way you did in freestyle, with one arm up and the other to your side. On the sideways drill, think of a snake wiggling through the water. Lift your head to breathe every four to six kicks.

Butterfly Pull

A good armstroke drill for butterfly is the one-arm

1. Your hands enter the water in front of your shoulders with your elbows bent slightly. Extend your arms as you catch the water. Keep your legs and feet together and kick down.

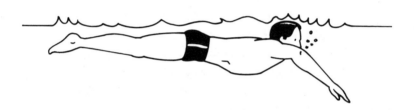

2. Pull your lower arms out with your thumbs tilted down. Bend your elbows, but keep them high, finishing the pull with your hands below your chest. Your head is now starting to come out of the water.

3. Kick again, pushing your hands back and out by your thighs. Raise your head and breathe in.

4. *Tuck your head forward and down after breathing, and bring your arms back to the front again. Keep your arms relaxed during recovery. As your hands enter the water for your second stroke, put your face back in the water, and begin another kick.*

pull with a dolphin kick. Concentrate on the timing of the kick—one kick with the arm in front and one with the arm in back.

You can also do what's called "single-single-double," or S-S-D. To do this, pull with one arm and breathe, pull with the other arm and breathe, and then pull butterfly with both arms without a breath. Other combinations include S-D-S-D (again, alternating arms on the single strokes), or S-D-D, or S-S-D-D. Experiment with different combinations of breathing patterns, sometimes breathing on the doubles rather than the singles. The single-double drills are great for helping you work on getting your shoulders out of the water.

Butterfly Breathing

Most butterfly swimmers breathe every two strokes but there may be times when you'll need to breathe every stroke. Breathing tends to make your hips sink, so breathing every two or three strokes helps you keep good form. Maintain your forward motion by sticking your chin out when your face comes up to breathe. Tuck your head back down again as your arms are about to enter the water.

Butterfly Turns

The one thing about butterfly that's easier than any other stroke is the turn. Touch the wall with both hands at the same time. Pull your feet up under you and plant them on the wall. Push off on your side and rotate to your stomach as you do two or three strong dolphin kicks before your first armstroke. Breathe on the second armstroke off the wall.

That's it—no flips, no pulldowns. Just turn, push and start swimming again.

Stroke Infractions

U.S. Swimming and FINA have established rules in the four strokes that everyone has to follow to be sure all races are fair. The best advice is to swim the strokes legally in practice so that you don't have to think about it when it's time for a race. Otherwise, a sharp-eyed referee will catch the mistake and you'll be DQ'd—disqualified.

Backstrokers have to stay on their backs for the entire race. That includes touching the wall at turns, pushing off after the turn, and finishing at the end of the race.

Butterflyers have to touch with two hands at the same time on every turn and at the finish. Your shoulders have to be even—one shoulder can't dip lower than the other as you come to the wall. The arms must move together. The legs have to stay together, too—no flutter kicking.

Breaststrokers also have to touch with two hands at the same time, keep their shoulders level and be careful not to dolphin kick. More swimmers get DQ'd for illegal dolphin kicks in breaststroke than for any other mistake except for false starting on a relay. It's most important to keep your legs from dolphin kicking during the underwater pulldown off the breaststroke start and turn.

Also on breaststroke, your head can go under the surface of the water but must break the surface once during every complete arm and leg stroke cycle.

Freestyle? Well there's not much you can do wrong except stop, stand up and push off the bottom of the pool to start swimming again. If you do stop, to get going again you have to "float forward" without pushing off the bottom. You can do any stroke you want in a freestyle race — even dogpaddle! But since the object is to swim as fast as possible, it's a real exception to see any stroke other than the crawl in a freestyle race.

Racing Starts

When you watch a championship swim meet on TV, the starts look pretty simple. The swimmers bend forward on the command "Take your mark" and dive in at the sound of the gun or horn.

If you tape one of these races and look at the start again, you'll see that each swimmer stands on the *starting block* slightly differently. After years of practice, each swimmer has discovered the best position for getting off the block and into the water with maximum speed.

Standing starts are used in freestyle, breaststroke and butterfly races. In these events, you stand on top of the block to start the race. Backstroke is the only stroke in which you start the race in the water.

The two types of standing starts are *grab starts* and *armswing starts*. Almost every beginner learns the armswing start first, and moves on to the grab start after getting some racing experience in meets. At top competitive levels, grab starts are used for all individual races and

49

for the lead-off leg in a freestyle relay. The other relay legs use armswing starts. We'll talk about why in a moment.

First, all race start diving should be in deep water. Six to eight feet is a recommended depth, but this isn't always possible at your local pool. Also, be sure that *all* of your race diving practice is under your coach's supervision. Diving in shallow water can cause serious injury.

Armswing Starts

Beginners learn the armswing start first because it gives the feeling of using your entire body to generate the push you need off the block. At the starting sound, swing your arms in a backward circle to help throw your arms out, back and around in front of you.

This backward circle does give you a more powerful push off the block. But your body hesitates a bit while your arms swing around, and this slows you down. Most top competitive swimmers use the grab start because there is no hesitation and it is therefore slightly faster.

If you're the second, third, or fourth leg of a relay, though, you should use the armswing start because you can begin the backward wind-up while the other swimmer is coming in. Start the wind-up when that swimmer is on the very last stroke into the wall. If you time it right, you will be pushing off and leaning forward into the air as the other swimmer touches. There should be no gap between the other swimmer's touch and your start. Once you're in the air, do the same kind of curve as described in the grab start below.

Grab Starts

In the grab start, the swimmer grabs the front of the

block between her feet with both hands. Notice that the feet are about shoulder width apart and the knees are bent slightly. Her head is down and she is looking at the water or block directly under her.

Some swimmers put their feet together and grab the block on either side of their feet. Some grip the block hard and others barely touch the block. Your coach can help you determine which arm and leg positions work best for you. Whichever you choose, always keep your body relaxed, your eyes open, and your ears tuned to the starter's command.

When the horn or gun sounds to start the race, pull or press against the front of the block with your hands. Lift your head forward quickly as your legs start their push. With your hands together, lift your arms straight out to a point directly under your head as you leave the block. Think of diving *up and out* rather than just out. By diving up and out, you curve through the air and dive farther from the block than you would by diving straight out at a flatter angle to the water surface.

As you curve through the air, bend at the hips. This keeps your legs up and behind you at the top of the curve. Put your hands together, squeeze your shoulders tightly against your ears, keep your head down, your legs straight at the knees, and your toes pointed.

Try to enter the water as smoothly as possible. Enter through a "doughnut hole." The object is to not let any part of your body touch the sides of the doughnut. You want your hands, head, body, legs and feet to enter cleanly.

Once you're in the water, stay streamlined as you curve back up toward the surface. There is a point underwater where you can tell that you are starting to slow down, and that is when you start swimming to keep your forward momentum going as much as possible. In breaststroke you begin your underwater pulldown when you start to slow down. In freestyle and butterfly, start kicking as soon as you dive in to keep your momentum up. This also helps your head and body pop up above the water. Then, start your armstroke. Get your shoulders up and out of the water to help you ride high from the very first stroke.

The *track start* is a slight variation of the grab start. It looks like the start runners use in track meets. To do this start, you put one foot on the block slightly behind the other, keeping your knees slightly bent. Some swimmers use this start because they can react to the starting gun or horn more quickly. Experiment. It may or may not work better for you.

Backstroke Starts

In backstroke races, you begin in the water, holding onto the block. Get into a crouched position. The USS rule is to put both feet against the wall so that the water just covers your toes. As long as both feet are under water, you can place your feet side by side or you can tuck one foot under the toes of the other. The rule on feet position varies some for high school and college meets, and your coach can explain the current rule for you.

For a USS backstroke start, tilt your head forward slightly. When you hear the starting sound, throw your head up and back. Throw your arms out and around parallel to the water to arch your body up and away from the block. Keep your elbows bent slightly.

Push off with your legs and get your hips up over the

water. Finish the push by extending your toes hard. Try to look for the other end of the pool when your head goes back during the leg-push. Finally, just like with the standing start, try to make a hole in the water with your hands and then go through the hole with your entire body. This is harder to do in backstroke than in a forward dive, but it's a goal you eventually want to reach.

Workouts

When you start competitive swimming, you'll soon find out that coaches rarely give you the same workout twice. There are some similarities, though, and there are several basic things you should know about how workouts are set up to help you become a better swimmer.

For the backstroke start in US swimming, your toes must be just under the surface of the water, and your head tilted slightly forward.

Before a workout begins, it's a good idea to do some easy stretching. Most important, swing your arms forward and backward. Swimming works your shoulders the hardest, so you want to warm up those muscles.

Now comes the swimming warm-up. Take it easy! The idea is to relax and concentrate on good stroke technique. If you have a choice of strokes, swim freestyle when you first get in. Save the other strokes for after you've swum a few laps. The warm-up helps you get your lungs working, your heart rate up and your muscles ready to begin the most important part of the workout, the *sets* or *repeats*.

Pushing off hard with your legs while throwing your arms out and head back will give you a strong backstroke start.

Keep in mind that when several people are sharing a swimming lane, you need to give each other plenty of room. Swim to the right of the line on the bottom of the pool. If you need to pass someone, touch his or her toes so the person will know to stop at the end and let you by. If your toes are touched, let the swimmer behind you pass. Another way to pass is for the slower swimmer to keep swimming to the outside of the lane while the faster swimmer passes up the middle.

Sets or *repeats* are usually the longest part of a workout. This is where you swim a certain distance in a certain amount of time over and over. Your coach will tell you what stroke you are swimming, and how far, how fast and how many times you will swim it. For example, you might repeat a set of five 25-yard freestyles on one minute–1:00. Or you might swim ten times 50-yard breaststroke on 1:45.

This is also called *interval training.* There's usually a big clock on the side of the pool for swimmers to watch so they know when to push off the wall. This is the *pace clock.* It has a minute hand and a second hand.

Say that you have four swimmers in your lane doing the set of five 25-yard freestyles. The first person starts when the second hand reaches the 60 at the top of the clock. The next swimmer will start five seconds after that, the third swimmer goes five seconds after the second swimmer, and the fourth swimmer goes five seconds after the third swimmer. When the first swimmer finishes her lap, she waits for the hand on the pace clock to hit 60 again. Then she starts her next 25-yard lap. Each swimmer repeats this five times.

Whether you're the first swimmer or the last swimmer,

your interval between each starting pushoff is always one minute. Don't get confused by the fact that you're leaving five, ten, or fifteen seconds after another swimmer. You will start each new 25-yard repeat one minute after the beginning of your last one.

Sets using interval training are usually the most tiring part of the workout. They work your muscles hard, sometimes to the point where you feel you can barely swim another stroke! But your muscles get stronger with rest, and that makes you able to go faster and farther in the future.

There are many, many different types of sets. Stroke drill sets can include kicking sets, pulling sets, or sets where you practice one specific part of a stroke. Sometimes they involve breath control practice, such as breathing every three strokes or every five strokes in freestyle.

Almost every workout will have a kicking set. That's because the leg muscles use almost half of the oxygen you consume but supply less than half of your actual speed.

It's easy to drag your legs during workout and then find in a race that they get tired very quickly. Coaches know this, so they usually include a kicking set to make sure everyone's legs get some work. Make your leg muscles *burn* during hard kicking sets.

Short distance repeats of 100 yards or less give you some rest between each repeat, but never enough, it seems. That's the point. You have to work your heart and lungs to the maximum. Your body is forced to recover quickly. Eventually you'll swim faster and faster using the same amount of effort.

Distance sets, where you're swimming repeats of 200 yards or longer, help you build endurance. The longer you're able to swim in practice without stopping to rest, the easier it'll be to swim those distances in a race without konking out after the first lap.

Most workouts include some sort of sprint work. These sets teach your muscles to react quickly, even after the stress of the earlier part of the workout. Sprints can be fun. They are often set up like relays. This gives you a chance to stand on the sidelines and yell encouragement to your teammates, because you'll probably get plenty of rest between each sprint.

After a workout, and even between sets, the coach will ask you to swim a few laps "easy." This is called the *warm-down* or sometimes, the *cool-down*. These laps allow your muscles to loosen up, which prevents soreness after the workout is over. The warm-down also helps your heart rate slow down gradually.

The warm-down can also help prevent cramps. You get a cramp when a muscle suddenly tightens up – sometimes into what feels like a knot – and causes a sharp pain. You get cramps in muscles that are not used to doing an exercise, when a muscle is tired, or when you swim in cold water. Cramps happen most often in the bottom of the foot, the calf of the lower leg, or the hamstring muscle located on the back of the upper leg. Cramps are usually caused by dehydration, so it's important to drink plenty of fluids before, during and after practice.

The best way to work a cramp out of your muscle is to stretch the muscle and continue to swim. For example, if your foot cramps, flex the foot and swim until the muscle relaxes. It may be uncomfortable at first, but eventually you'll "swim the cramp out." In the worst cases, you might have to stop and rub the muscle to help it relax.

Chapter 2

SWIMMING— MEET TIME!

Well, hotshot, here you are. You're standing at the edge of the starting block. Right in front of you is a big pool of water. The crowd that was just clapping and yelling like crazy suddenly gets quiet. All eyes are on you as the starter blows a whistle to get the timers ready.

So O.K. Let's show them what you can do. One last deep

In competition, the racer's edge starts with the dive off the

breath and it's time to go! Now you're pushing off for your dive, giving it everything you've got. The next sensation you feel is a great big SPLASH. You use every ounce of energy to ride high through your swim. And, hey, before you know it, it's all over. You did it.

And there goes that crowd again—clapping and yelling

starting block.

like crazy! Can you imagine all that happening to you?

This chapter will look at two kinds of meets that you'll compete in as an age-grouper. The first is a *dual meet,* where two teams swim against each other in the same pool at the same time. Dual meets usually last two to three hours. The team that scores the most points wins. The other is a *championship* or *invitational* meet. This is where more than two teams compete over one or more days.

Dual Meet Race Distances

For 8-and-unders, most races are only one length of a 25-yard pool. In the 9-10 and 11-12 age groups, each race is 50 yards or more. For 13-14 and 15-16 age groups, swimmers race for 100 yards and longer.

Most summer recreation league dual meets are held in 25-yard or 25-meter pools. The order of races, or events, can be different in every summer league program, but we'll use the following format for this example:

| | | DISTANCE IN YARDS | | | | |
| | | 8 and | | | | |
EVENT	AGE	under	9-10	11-12	13-14	15-17
1) Medley Relay		100	200	200	200	400
2) Freestyle		25	50	50	100	100
3) Individual Medley ..		100	100	200	200	200
4) Diving						
5) Breaststroke		25	50	50	100	100
6) Backstroke		25	50	50	100	100
7) Butterfly...........		25	50	50	100	100
8) Freestyle Relay		100	200	200	200	400

In each event, the 8-and-unders go first and the 15-16 age group goes last. In all age group meets, boys swim against boys, and girls against girls.

Notice event three. That's the *individual medley*, or "I.M." Medley means a combination of several things. In swimming, the I.M. is a race that combines all four strokes: butterfly, backstroke, breaststroke and freestyle.

Also notice that there are spots in the order for diving and relays. More on those events later.

What Happens in a Meet

For this example, let's call your team the Red Tornadoes and the other team the Blue Devils. The meet against the Blue Devils takes place on Saturday morning at your pool, so you're the home team.

All of your teammates have their red racing suits on and are wearing red team t-shirts on the pool deck. The other team is dressed in blue.

There will be two swimmers from your team against two from their team in each age group. First place in each race will get five points, second place will get three points, third place will get one point, and fourth place will not score. Each swimmer can compete for points in two events and two relays.

Your races will be the 50-yard freestyle and 50-yard breaststroke, and you will swim another 50-yard freestyle as part of your age group's freestyle relay.

You will also swim *exhibition* (non-scoring) in the 50-yard backstroke. That makes three events for you in this meet, but you're not breaking the two-event rule since your third event is non-scoring.

Why has your coach entered you exhibition in the backstroke when you don't have a chance? Well, your backstroke has been getting better and better in practice, and the coach wants you to swim it in race conditions to see how fast you can go.

Your club has a six-lane, 25-yard pool. The starting block end of the pool is 3½ feet deep. The bottom slopes gradually to 5½ feet halfway across, and then dips to 12 feet under the far end, where the 1-meter and 3-meter diving boards are located.

When the race begins, each racer has to swim alone with her

Meet Warm-up

The coach will ask all swimmers to be at the pool an hour before the meet for warm-up and the team meeting. The warm-up is as important on the day of the meet as it is in practice. It's your last chance to practice your stroke, starts and turns.

The last thing you'll do in your warm-up is swim one-lap sprints. It helps everyone get used to swimming fast and it gets your heart and lungs going.

own best efforts and her determination to win.

During the team meeting, your coach says the Reds and the Blues are very evenly matched, and the meet could be very close. Every swim is important for the team score. Your coach reminds you to think about what you've learned in workouts. He or she will remind a few individuals of particular things to be aware of during their races. Then the coach will lead a team cheer as a final "psych-up" before the start of the first event.

"Take Your Mark!"

Since your first event is the 50-yard freestyle, you can watch most of the medley relays and cheer for the Reds. Once the 13-14-year-old relays begin, you should start getting ready to go behind the blocks.

Often there will be two or three rows of chairs lined up behind each lane for the swimmers to sit in before their races. When there are rows of chairs like this, the swimmers move forward one chair as each race starts. There also may be a long bench behind the blocks. It's called the "ready bench," because that's where you sit when you're getting ready to swim.

The meet officials dress in white. First, there's the *starter.* He or she tells the swimmers to step up on the blocks. When all the swimmers are ready, the starter says, "Take your mark." Each swimmer has to get into position for his or her starting dive and remain perfectly still. Once the starter sees that everyone is still, the starter will fire the gun or sound the horn.

Most dual meets have two *stroke and turn judges.* One judge stands at the far end of the pool. He or she will be on the lookout for things like one-hand touches in breaststroke or butterfly, and swimmers turning over on their stomachs before touching the wall in a backstroke race. The meet starter often serves as a second stroke and turn judge, watching the front half of the pool.

Your coach says to remember to reach all the way in front of you on the armstroke, to push hard off the wall after your freestyle flip turn, and to kick hard as you get close to the finish. Then your coach gives you one quick handshake for good luck.

Your Race

There's only one thing you have any control over during your race, and that's how *you* swim. A lot of swimmers worry about what the other swimmers in a race are going to do, especially if they think the other swimmers are faster. But there's not a thing you can do about someone else's speed. When you're in the water, the only one you're competing against is yourself.

Once you're in the water, the only thing you want to think about is going as fast as you can.

Just before you step on the block for your first race, swing your arms a bit to stay loose. Jump up and down two or three times, pushing off the deck hard with your toes. That'll help you get ready for a strong push off the block on the start. Check your goggles to be sure they're tight. Boys should be sure their suits are tied tightly, because an untied suit could come off when you dive into the pool!

Now let's say that you've already swum the 50-yard freestyle and scored some points for the Reds. You were breathing hard after the race, but your heartbeat got back to normal pretty quickly.

Your lungs feel good now. Your arms and legs feel loose. When you check back with your coach after the swim, he or she tells you, "Good race. Your hips are still wiggling a bit too much from side to side, but we'll work on that next week in practice. You might think about that before the freestyle relay, but if you swim the same it'll be fine. Now get ready for the 50 breast."

Saving Energy Between Races

You're feeling really happy about scoring points in the freestyle, and you want to jump up and down to celebrate with your friends. Some of them may have finished all the races they will swim today, and they are yelling with excitement. But you shouldn't begin celebrating yet.

Jumping around is a distraction to your coach and other swimmers who are trying to concentrate on their own races. And too much carrying on wastes energy you might need in your later swims. Cheering for your teammates during their races is a positive action. Horseplay is negative. There'll be plenty of time to play around once the meet is over. But during the meet, keep focused on what's most important for both you and your team: Swimming well.

Since you still have other races, forget about the one you just swam and concentrate on the next one. There may be some things you weren't happy with, like running into the lane rope, but there's nothing you can do now to change what just happened. Think positive about your 50 breast.

A lot of kids snack during meets. As long as you don't overdo it, it's all right. The best snacks are bananas, oranges and grapes. Keep sweets to a minimum and don't eat anything within 15 minutes of your race. Fruit juices, noncarbonated "energy replacement" drinks and good old plain water are the best liquids to drink.

Your breaststroke race was fine, even though you finished fourth behind your teammate and the two Blue swimmers, and didn't score. You've decided to do even better in the backstroke, even if you won't be scoring points in it.

Now let's say the 50 backstroke race is over. You had a good backstroke start, kept your shoulders high in the water, and wound up finishing third overall, behind one Blue Devil and one of your Red teammates. Your coach was happy and said you'd definitely get to swim backstroke on some medley relays later this summer.

This Canadian racer rides high as he finishes the recovery for his breaststroke.

Relays

Even though most swimmers belong to teams, swimmers compete one at a time and don't depend on each other for teamwork the way players on a basketball or volleyball team do.

Relays are the one time when swimmers really feel part of a team sport. You have four swimmers on a relay team, and it's easier to get psyched up when you have others to help out.

Even though relays set one team against another, it's important for you to swim your own race and not worry about who you're swimming against. Bruce Hayes has some good advice. He was on the United States men's 800-meter freestyle relay team that won a gold medal in the 1984 Olympics—by 4/100 of a second! Says Bruce, "It's important to always swim your own race, whether you're ahead or behind. The lead can change several times in a relay. I'm sure we wouldn't have won the race if I hadn't stuck to my own race plan."

On a *freestyle relay,* each person (or *leg*) swims freestyle. A *medley relay* has a different person swimming each of the four strokes: the backstroker leads off, followed by the breaststroker, butterflyer, and freestyler.

Teamwork comes into play on relays during the exchanges. The *exchange* is the part of a relay when one swimmer touches the wall and the next swimmer dives from the block to start swimming.

It's important to wait for the swimmer ahead of you to actually *touch* before you dive. You can be swinging your arms for the take-off, but your feet must stay in contact with the starting block until the swimmer before you

Body roll is important in the back stroke. This swimmer's right shoulder comes out of the water as he recovers with his right arm.

touches. That makes it a *legal exchange*. If you make an *illegal exchange* and leave the block before the touch, your relay team will be disqualified by the judges.

Disqualifications happen to every team at some point, but it's important to practice exchanges so your team doesn't get disqualified. Winning relays in dual meets usually score seven points, and second place scores no points. If your relay wins, you'll help your team in the overall scoring a lot.

Keep your part of an exchange safe. Be sure the swimmer ahead of you is about to touch before you start your dive from the block. When you're finishing, swim hard into the wall, so the next swimmer doesn't have to guess when you will touch.

Relays are often the most thrilling parts of a meet. If a race is close, and the crowd and the opposing teams are all cheering, relay swimmers may get so excited they swim faster than they did during their individual races.

It turns out that your freestyle relay race *was* one of those exciting races. All four legs were neck-and-neck, but the Blue Devils' last swimmer pulled ahead at the end of the last lap. The Blue Devils were jumping up and down, happy to have won. And while all four members of your team feel like they swam well, you're all disappointed about the loss.

Your coach says everything's O.K., though, because you'll have another chance to swim against the same Blue Devils relay team in the league invitational championship at the end of the season. With hard work and practice to make your exchanges a little bit faster, you just might beat them the next time.

Besides, the Red Tornadoes scored enough points in the other races to win the meet. After a quick jump into the pool with your coach, everyone's going out to celebrate with a big pizza lunch. And after a meet, your appetite will probably be enormous!

Championship Meets

The second type of meet you'll swim in is a *championship* or *invitational* meet. There can be any number of teams participating. It's called an invitational because many teams are invited to compete. It can become a championship meet if all of your summer league teams are competing to determine the overall winner for the season.

The order of events at an invitational meet may be similar to the order in a dual meet. Usually, though, there are additional races at longer or shorter distances in each age group for each stroke. You will be allowed to swim more events than you can in a dual meet.

At an invitational meet, there will be a lot of swimmers entered in each event. If the meet is being held in an 8-lane pool, but 14 swimmers are entered in the 100-yard butterfly, then meet organizers will divide the swimmers into two *heats*. Six swimmers will race in Heat 1, and eight swimmers will swim in Heat 2.

How do they decide which swimmers will be in each heat? A few weeks before the invitational meet, each coach sent in an *entry form* listing which events each of his team members would swim. Next to the event, your coach listed an *entry time,* sometimes called a *seed time.* This time can be either your fastest time ever in that event, or the coach's best guess as to what time you will swim in the event during the invitational meet. If you've never swum the event in a meet before, the coach may enter you as "N.T." This stands for "No Time."

When the officials receive the entry forms from every team in the meet, they sort the entry times for each event from fastest to slowest. All N.T. entries are sorted with the slowest times. This is called *seeding.* The fastest swimmers are seeded into the last heat of an event.

Swimmers are assigned lanes according to their seed times. In the 100-yard butterfly, for example, the fastest swimmers will be assigned the middle lanes of the pool in the last heat. They will be in lanes four and five of the eight-lane pool. The next fastest swimmers will be in lanes three and six. The next swimmers will be in lanes two and seven, and then lanes one and eight.

The other six swimmers will be seeded in Heat 1 according to their entry times in the same way, from the middle lanes on out. In Heat 1, the outside lanes one and eight will be empty during the race. In some meets, the fastest swimmers compete in the first heat and other heats have the next-fastest swimmers. But most invitational meets run the heats from slow to fast.

At some invitational meets, swimmers will compete in *preliminaries* and *finals*. During the preliminaries, or "prelims," swimmers compete in the heats of each event to qualify among the top six or eight times. During the finals, these fastest swimmers race again to determine the final placings. The prelims usually take place in the morning and the finals take place that same day in the evening. Meets with prelims and finals are often spread out over four days or more. The Junior Olympics, the USS National Championships, and the Olympics all have prelims and finals.

Most invitational meets, however, are shorter and have heats called *timed finals*. During timed finals, you swim each race only once to determine your place in the final standings. At these meets, there is usually a limit on the number of individual events and relays you are allowed to swim each day.

Sometimes, a swimmer may decide not to go to a meet after he or she has entered. Or sometimes your coach may decide to hold you out of a race to save energy for a later race. If a swimmer fails to show up when it's time for his

A powerful butterfly gives competitive swimmers a sense of exhilaration unmatched by any other stroke.

or her heat to swim, the swimmer is *scratched* from the race. There is usually no penalty for scratching a race, but you and your coach should let the meet officials know if you need to scratch a race for any reason. It helps the officals run the meet more efficiently.

You may wait several hours between swims. If there's a separate pool for warm-ups between races, jump in and swim a few laps—especially if you have to wait more than an hour between races. It's very important to get your heart and lungs going again, particularly if you've had a nap. You should also use the other pool to warm down after you finish your races.

Be sure to drink water and other fluids at these meets. When you swim, it's very easy to get dehydrated without realizing it. A good rule is to drink some water whenever you pass a fountain. Also, try to space out whatever you eat during the day so that your food is digested and settled long before your next race.

When your event is called, you may have to pick up an *entry card* from the *clerk of the course*. The clerk of the course sits at a table on the pool deck or in an office, and has entry cards arranged with each swimmer's name, seed time, and lane assignment. At some meets, you will be required to pick this card up and give it to the timers behind your lane right before you get on the block to swim. At other meets, an official may hand the cards to the timers so that the swimmers don't have to worry about them.

After the race, the timer writes your time on the entry card and hands it to the *runner*. The runner collects the cards after every heat and takes them to the *meet scorer*, who figures out where each swimmer placed in the event and how many points were scored for each team.

If you finished in the top six or eight, you might win a ribbon. If you score in the top three in your event, you might win a medal. If your team scores in the top three overall, the team might win a trophy!

Ribbons, medals and trophies sure are nice to look at when you get home. But the best part about a meet comes right after your swims, when you realize your hard work in practice has paid off with fast times.

Swimming Camps

There are many opportunities for young swimmers to attend camps to improve their swimming abilities, especially during the summer. Many coaches offer private instruction for various lengths of time, either over a weekend or sometimes for a week or two. Your coach and parents can find many of these camps advertised in *Swimming World* magazine, and they can help you find a good program.

United States Swimming also sponsors local training seminars that range from a half-day to a week. These programs operate in inner-city areas, suburbs and in the countryside. They include stroke classes, motivation sessions and goal setting. Your coach may already know about USS camps in your area, or you can write for more information to:

United States Swimming
1750 E. Boulder St.
Colorado Springs, CO 80909

Chapter 3

DIVING—
FIRST APPROACH

*C*ompetitive diving actually has more in common with gymnastics, ballet and circus acrobatics than it does with swimming! Gymnasts do somersaults, twists and handstands during their routines. Circus clowns and acrobats are masters at tumbling and—very important—they know how to fall safely. Ballet and jazz dancers learn grace and good posture, which are similar to what judges look for in good divers. You will learn a lot about these skills in a good competitive diving program.

Diving Safety

Many people have the mistaken belief that diving is a dangerous sport and that accidents are common. This is simply not true if you train and compete in a supervised program. There is no record of a death or catastrophic injury in more than 80 years of competitive diving programs in the United States.

The key word here is "competitive." Competitive diving programs are supervised by coaches, and safety is the number one priority in competitive diving. Sometimes you will read or hear about someone diving into the surf at the beach or into a pool and becoming paralyzed with a spinal cord injury (SCI). These accidents almost always are the result of horseplay or carelessness. In swimming pools, accidents almost always happen in shallow water, not the deep end where competitive diving takes place.

Most SCI diving accidents happen to young men between ages 13 and 24. At least half of these victims have also been drinking alcoholic beverages prior to the accident. One study showed that these accidents occur in water four feet deep or less, more than half occur during

After years of training, a good diver can make difficult dives look graceful and much easier than they really are.

or after sundown, and the victim usually claims he couldn't see the bottom. The people involved are usually not divers, have little or no formal diving training, and are not being properly supervised when the accidents happen.

As you can see, these accidents have nothing to do with competitive diving workouts or diving meets. Although the risk in diving, as in other sports, is ever-present, the safety record for competitive diving in the United States is first rate. It's important for you and your parents to know that supervised competitive diving is no riskier than many other sports.

The supervision provided by a qualified diving coach is a major factor in competitive diving's excellent safety record. The information presented here is not intended as a substitute for a diving coach. If you are interested in competitive diving, first locate a coach to instruct you safely.

For example, coaches in competitive diving programs teach safe water entry techniques. You learn how to move in the air so that you *won't* hurt yourself when you hit the water. Most accidents happen when a person's head hits the bottom. But coaches teach divers how to steer up after they enter the water.

Competitive divers train and compete in the deep area of a pool. The American Red Cross recommends that you learn your first dives into water at least nine feet deep. In U.S. Diving competitions, you will dive into water at least 11 feet deep under the 1-meter springboard and 12 feet deep under the 3-meter springboard.

Divers practice body alignment drills on land and into pools to learn to make their bodies rigid to protect them-

A back dive in a straight position. Correct body alignment is not only necessary to score points — it's safer as well.

selves from injury. For correct body alignment in competitive diving, you will learn to rotate your hips under your shoulders so that your upper body and lower body are in a straight line, which protects your lower back. Incorrect entries, whether occasional or repeated, can also cause injuries to your wrists and shoulders. With practice on body alignment and what's called "position sense" in the air, you will gradually learn skills to reduce the risk of these injuries.

Age, muscle and bone strength, skill and experience also have a lot to do with diving safety. As you get older, stronger and more experienced, you will progress from the 1-meter board to the 3-meter board, and perhaps even to the 10-meter platform. The higher the board, the faster you travel through the air and the harder you hit the water. Because young divers' bodies are still growing and developing strength, there are no competitions for the 13 and under age group from the 10-meter platform.

Diving History

Many historical references to diving are part of battle stories, describing soldiers and warriors diving into water to escape their enemies. But recreational diving—diving for fun—first developed in the early 1800s as an outgrowth of gymnastics. The Swedes turned it into a competitive sport in the late 1800s, and it was soon adopted as a sport by the English as well.

Stunt diving received most of the attention in the early years of diving as a sport. People would bet on how high someone could dive or jump into the water and survive. A widely publicized dive occurred in 1871 when a man dived from the London Bridge.

Just as daring, Hawaiian natives became known for diving from high, rocky cliffs into deep water. In 1918, Alex Wickham of the Solomon Islands dived more than 200 feet (a 20-story building!) off an Australian cliff. He blacked out during the fall and lost his bathing suit from the force of his landing. His body was black and blue all over for weeks, but he lived.

But hey, kids, don't try this at home!

Diving as an acrobatic sport became part of the 1904 Olympics in St. Louis. Standards for judging diving were hotly argued. Americans emphasized the quality of the entry into the water. The Germans did more difficult moves in the air but often landed on their chests and stomachs. As diving became more and more popular around the world in later years, both the acrobatics in the air and the entry into the water became important in judging a dive.

American divers have dominated world competition since 1920. The youngest American champion was Marjorie Gestring, who was only 13 years and 9 months old when she won the 3-meter springboard at the 1936 Olympics in Berlin. Korean-American Sammy Lee won the 10-meter platform in both the 1948 and 1952 Olympics. Pat McCormick won both the 3-meter springboard and 10-meter platform titles at both the 1952 and 1956 Olympics. And Greg Louganis won five World Championship titles and five Olympic medals during his career. After winning a silver in the 10-meter platform event at the 1976 Olympics, Greg won double gold medals on the 3-meter springboard and 10-meter platform at the 1984 and 1988 Olympics.

Greg is frequently called the greatest diver of all time because he did the most difficult dives with such beauty that they looked easy. Greg jumped higher, looked more graceful in the air and "ripped his entries" better than any of his competitors.

Other great divers have come from Mexico, the Soviet Union, Italy, Germany, and Sweden. During the 1980s, the Chinese began to rival and in some cases surpass American divers in international competition.

In the pike position, a diver bends her body at the hips but keeps her legs straight at the knees. This is an open pike position, because her arms are extended away from her body.

U.S. Diving sets rules for American diving the same way U.S. Swimming does for American swimming. The national championships sponsored by U.S. Diving have competitions in the 1-meter and 3-meter springboards and the 10-meter tower. The Junior Olympic competitions include the 5-meter and 7.5-meter platforms as well. U.S. Diving also publishes manuals on diving safety.

U.S. Diving, like U.S. Swimming, is a member of FINA. FINA maintains international standards for competitive diving and conducts the diving competitions at the Olympics Games. FINA also conducts a World Championship diving meet two years after every Summer Olympics. Like the Olympics, the World Championship diving events are the 3-meter springboard and the 10-meter platform.

Diving competitions are also held as a part of summer swimming league programs. Many high schools and some junior high schools have diving teams. Most school teams compete on 1-meter springboards. The more advanced school *programs* offer instruction in 3-meter springboard and 5-, 7.5- and 10-meter platform.

The NCAA supervises diving at the collegiate level. In college meets, points are scored on 1-meter and 3-meter springboards, and on the 10-meter tower at championship meets.

Diving has progressed and changed a great deal since the early 1900s. At one point, there were just 14 platform and 20 springboard dives. There are now more than 60 possible dives in each event. In 1904, a forward double somersault dive from the platform was considered dangerous, but today many senior divers complete perfect inward 3½ somersault dives from the platform. As training methods improve, standards of excellence continue to evolve for all age groups in competitive diving.

Jump High and Rip!

Champion divers sometimes make a sound when they enter the water perfectly. It sounds like a piece of paper being ripped in two. This is called a *rip entry*.

That's what the term "rip" means. One of the skills in competitive diving is to learn to rip your entries without a splash. To do that, you have to be properly aligned straight up and down and as rigid as possible as you approach the water. Place or grab your hands in a flat, blunt shape. Raise your shoulders high and lock your elbows to make your body as long as possible.

Speed is an important part of a rip entry. It's actually easier to rip your entry the higher you dive because you'll be travelling faster when you hit the water.

Eager to start? Let's assume you already know how to dive from the pool deck. Your teachers have had you jump from a 1-meter diving board feet first. You've probably gone off the 1-meter board head first, and perhaps you've even jumped off a 3-meter board feet first or dived head first a few times.

But even if you've never done these things, competitive diving is a fun sport. It's a part of many summer swimming and diving programs, and many kids start diving in these programs. Some kids continue to train during the fall, winter and spring after school with other community teams or at the YMCA or YWCA. You can attend state and regional diving meets, and many age group divers set goals of scoring enough points in these meets to qualify for the annual Junior Olympic competitions.

Concentration is as important as skill in learning to dive correctly.

Boards and Platforms

Springboards are the standard diving boards that bounce up and down. Under the springboard is a moveable lever called a *fulcrum,* which you can adjust to give the board more or less bounce. You may have to adjust the wheel of the fulcrum with your hands. Or you may be able to adjust it with your feet while you hold onto a rail attached to the board.

The 1-meter springboard is frequently called the "low board," and the 3-meter springboard is called the "high board."

The 1-meter springboard isn't located 1 meter off the ground. Rather, it's 1 meter from the tip of the board straight down to the surface of the water. The distance to the water from the 3-meter board and platforms is measured the same way. This straight line from the tip of the board to the water surface is the *plummet line.*

Platforms don't bounce. They're often made of concrete with a non-slip surface on top. They're either 5 meters, 7.5 meters or 10 meters high. At some pools, 1-meter and 3-meter platforms are also used to learn basic skills. You may sometimes hear the term "tower diving." That's because the big structure or pedestal holding the various platforms is known as the *tower.*

Dive Groups

Now let's break diving down into the different types of dives. There are four main groups, the *forward, backward, inward* and *reverse* dives. Each of these four types can be performed in one of three positions, either *straight, pike,* or *tuck.* If you add one or more somersaults, you can see there are a lot of possibilities for some pretty fancy dives!

There is also a fifth type of dive, the *twisting* dive. Twisting dives can be performed on forward, backward, inward and reverse dives, and they are done in the *free* position, which is a combination of straight, pike or tuck positions.

From the platform, there is a sixth dive group, the *armstand*. In an armstand dive, you start a dive by balancing in an armstand (sometimes called a handstand) at the end of the platform.

The Forward Dive Group

There are five steps to a forward dive—*approach, hurdle, take-off, flight* and *entry*.

The *approach* is your walk from your starting position to the end of the board.

The jump you take from one foot to two feet at the end of the board to start the board bouncing is called the *hurdle*. Divers have to jump high to get as much spring from the board as possible.

You have to take at least three steps in the approach before the hurdle, although you can take more. You'll figure out where to start your approach on your pool's board, and with which foot to take the first step. When you compete at another pool on an unfamiliar board, you can figure out where to start by simply walking to the end of the board, turning around, and doing your normal approach toward the fulcrum. Where you land after your hurdle is where you'll start your approach. There are usually markings or numbers on the side of the board to help you remember your starting spot.

The judges start thinking about your score as soon as

Approach

Hurdle

Take Off

The diving hurdle is performed in one smooth motion. The higher you jump when you begin your hurdle, the more spring you'll get from the diving board.

you start your approach. You have to make your approach smooth and without any hesitation, and you have to maintain proper body alignment. Your arms and hands should be straight, but not too stiff. Relax your shoulder and neck muscles so you can swing your arms comfortably.

Right before the hurdle, your arms may swing slightly behind you. Swing your arms forward and up as one knee lifts for the hurdle. It doesn't matter which knee you lift. You'll figure out which one is more natural for you.

Jump up off the other foot, pushing strongly against the board.

It's important that you hurdle straight up to carry you forward, not backward. Keep your shoulders and hips lined up straight. Be sure that you can see the end of the board during the approach and hurdle.

Now you're ready for the *take-off*. Touch down on both feet at the end of the hurdle to give the board its final, biggest bounce. Actively push downward against the board with your legs by squatting slightly. Then, extend your legs to go up. The spring you get on the take-off lifts you into the air for the flight.

The *flight* is the path you take when you're moving through the air. What you do during the flight is the actual *dive*. The dive can be plain, like a forward dive in the straight position. Or it can be fancy, like a forward with 2½ somersaults in the tuck position.

Ride time occurs after the hurdle. It's the amount of time between the hurdle touchdown on two feet until the instant you take off. In general, the stronger you push against the board on your touchdown, the more the board will bend and the longer you ride time will be. When you watch competitive diving on TV, the announcers will often say that a diver "rode the board." That means the diver got strong push after her touchdown.

The extra time you "hang in the air" when you have a strong, high take-off is your hang time. Whenever you successfully ride the board, chances are your hang time will be very good, too. The higher you can spring into the air from your take-off, the more time in the air you have to travel away from the board and complete your dive before passing the board on your way back down.

Most of your workouts will involve learning new positions, somersaults and twists you'll use in the air. The ride time for every dive in the forward dive group should be approximately the same, regardless of how many

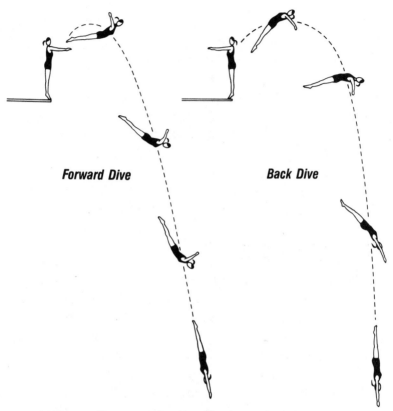

Forward Dive   **Back Dive**

A dive from each of the four main groups is shown in different stages of flight. All dives are in the straight position.

somersaults and twists you do.

Finally, the *entry*. When you enter the water, you want to be almost straight up and down (near-vertical) with your toes pointed. If you enter head first, you should stretch your arms over your head in a straight line with your body. Your hands should be flat, grabbed or close together to help you rip it. If you land feet first, hold your arms straight to your sides.

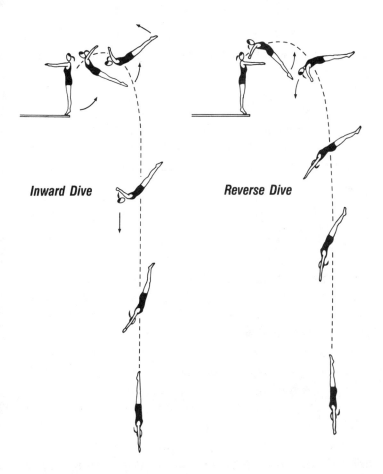

Inward Dive

Reverse Dive

"Near-vertical" means as close to vertical as possible. Very few dives are absolutely straight up and down, although that is the illusion you want to create. Dives that aren't vertical are either over-rotated or under-rotated. When you over-rotate a dive, you've gone "past vertical." When you under-rotate a dive, you're "short." For the ideal near-vertical entry, aim to be a tiny bit short, not past vertical.

In both the forward and backward dive groups, you rotate forward away from the board in the same direction as your flight path.

The Back Dive Group

To start a back dive, stand near the back of the board or fulcrum and walk to the tip. This is not the same as a forward dive's approach, and it doesn't matter how many steps you take. But you do want to appear relaxed and confident.

When you get to the tip, turn around and raise your arms to shoulder level to help you balance. Slide your feet backward, one at a time, until your heels are extended over the edge of the board. You should be standing on the balls of your feet. Bring your heels together. After you're securely balanced, you may leave your arms up or bring your hands back down to your side to assume your starting position.

Now you're ready for the back dive *press*. Your ankles have to "prime" the board by making it vibrate up and down slightly. On the last "prime," raise your arms up and extend your body up on your toes as much as possible. Without your toes leaving the board, drop your heels and push down strongly on the board as you squat. Then extend your body during take-off.

The back press on a backstanding take-off does the same thing as the hurdle on a forward approach. You squat in both positions, and that pushes the board down. A strong press will increase your ride time when the board recoils.

There are two skills you will learn that are particularly important for doing dives in the back group. One

A diver prepares to begin her back dive press. Her arms are extended to help her maintain her balance while she is standing on the balls of her feet.

is learning to *spot* the board in front with your eyes while you rotate backward. Spotting is discussed below.

Another skill that helps you do back dives with 1½ or 2½ somersaults in tuck position is the *kick-out.* A kick-out is when you come out of a spin by extending your legs first, instead of your head. The kickout slows the speed of your rotation.

The Inward Dive Group

Inward dives start in the same position as back dives, with you balanced on the balls of your feet at the end of the board. This time, after the take-off, you'll rotate forward toward the board and opposite the direction of the flight path. An inward dive is a forward dive you perform by starting in the back dive position.

The Reverse Dive Group

The inward and reverse dives are similar because in both groups you rotate toward the board, opposite the direction of the flight path. A reverse dive starts with the same approach, hurdle, and take-off as a forward dive. During the flight, though, your body changes direction and you rotate backward toward the board rather than forward away from the board. In other words, it's a back dive you complete by starting from a forward take-off.

Reverse dives are the most difficult of the basic four to learn. Finishing your dive in the air and making a good near-vertical entry on a reverse dive is harder because you have to change direction in mid-air. You get a tremendous sense of accomplishment the first time you complete a reverse dive.

Dive Positions

On each of the above four groups of dives, you can do dives with either no somersaults or with up to 3½ somersaults. A few of the very best divers perform forward 4½ somersaults from the 10-meter platform in competition.

A somersault is one full rotation of your body either forward or backward. Somersaults with full rotations end with your feet going into the water first. When you do somersaults with 1½, 2½, 3½ and 4½ rotations, you'll enter the water head first.

In addition, you can dive in one of these three positions:

• *Straight position.* Keep your body straight, with no bending at the knees or hips. Your legs are held together and your toes are pointed. Depending upon the dive, your arms will be either at your side pressed against your body, or, during the basic dive in each dive group, stretched out sideways during the flight through the air.

After "priming" the board, the diver begins her press for the back dive. A strong press will increase the diver's ride time.

Basic Body Positions

Pike

Tuck

Straight

• *Pike position.* Bend your body at the hips, but keep your legs straight at the knees. Point your toes, and hold your legs as close to your chest as possible. In *open pike* the arms are extended sideways. In *closed pike* the hands reach and grab behind the legs slightly below the knees.

• *Tuck position.* Bend your body at the knees and hips, as if you are curling into a ball. Again, keep your knees and feet together with toes pointed and try to make the tuck as tight as possible.

It's easier to spin faster and do more somersaults in the tuck position than in the pike position, and easier in the pike than straight position. You'll also find it easier sometimes to complete the number of somersaults by spreading your knees into a split tuck and holding them even tighter against your chest. During competition, splitting your *tucks* in any position is an error and judges will take one or two points off your score.

Twisting Dives Group

Twisters can start from either the forward approach or the back dive position. A twist means spinning around once in a full circle. A half-twist is a half-circle. On forward dives, you can twist any number of times from ½ twist, which is the easiest, to 3 twists. You can also twist while doing 1½ or 2½ somersaults. Add the straight, pike, tuck or free position and you've got a lot of possible twisting combinations.

If you do a forward dive with ½ twist, you will enter the water facing the same direction from your take-off but upside down. That holds true for 1½ and 2½ twists, too. On 1, 2 or 3 twists, your entry will be opposite the direction of your take-off.

Learning to Spot

Once airborne, divers have to know which way is up and which way is down. The best way to keep from "getting lost" in a dive is to learn to *spot* the dive.

To spot, you find a place to look, and then you use that spot as a guide to know when to kick out and extend your body before entering the water. You must learn to *open your eyes* to see the spot even though you are somersaulting or twisting.

Here's the basic guideline for spotting. On front, inward, reverse and twisting dives, spot the water. On back dives, spot the board. It's not a good idea to spot a wall or another object at your home pool because a similar object may not be there when you are diving in another pool. You can spot the board and water because they will always be in the same place.

You will eventually develop a "feeling" for when it is time to open up from your somersaults or twists. You will learn to feel your position and combine that with spotting to be sure you enter the water straight up and down. Being aware at all times how your body moves through the air during the flight is called *position sense*. In some dives, you will spot before you kick out. During practice, your coach may call out something like "Now!" to help you learn when you should see your spot before entry.

There are several exercises you can do on land to help you learn to spot. First, balance on your tiptoes, and then balance on the toes of one foot. Try it with your eyes open, and then try it with your eyes closed. Next, jump up and keep your body straight.

Now comes the spotting. Mark a spot on the floor about 16 or 17 feet away. Jump and do a half turn, and then do a full turn, both to the left and to the right. Keep your head forward and watch the spot as long as possible as you twist, and then snap your head around and find the spot again as your body turns. Try doing this slowly or fast, and try different combinations of half or full twists going both left and right.

A good way to practice feeling and spotting is to jump and spin with your eyes closed. How closely can you come to twisting back to the spot you chose earlier? Open your eyes and repeat the same jump.

Spotting becomes more and more useful as you learn difficult dives. Through practice, spotting will eventually become automatic for you. Your coach won't have to help by calling out to you from the pool deck, because your position sense in each dive will help you feel when to spot.

Other Diving Training

Divers practice many skills to develop strength, flexibility, concentration and control. Much of a diver's training involves simply getting on the springboard and diving into the water.

Diving coaches frequently talk about *skill progressions.* A skill progression is a series of skills you learn, starting with the most simple and gradually becoming more advanced. Simpler skills usually form the basics of the advanced skills. That's why you learn them first. In diving, the simpler skills include dives and basic gymnastics moves. These are called *core skills.* Intermediate level dives are called *lead-up skills.* The most advanced dives are called *complex skills.*

Core skills are the diving basics. They include body alignment, correct toe point, vertical entry into the water, forward, back, reverse and inward dives in tuck and pike positions from the springboards, forward and backward rolls on gymnastic mats, armstands on the ground, and forward handsprings. Once you have mastered these, you will be ready for the intermediate level.

Lead-ups are dives that, once mastered, "lead up" to complex diving skills. Forward, backward, inward and reverse dives in straight position are intermediate level

103

lead-up dives. So are 1½ somersaults in pike and tuck positions in all four directions. For advanced divers, an armstand somersault on the 3- or 5-meter platform is a lead-up dive. You would learn it before moving up to doing armstand somersaults from the 7.5- and 10-meter platforms.

Complex dives include two or more somersaults in tuck or pike position in any of the four directions, and dives with one or more twists. Again, your coach will help you decide when you are ready to practice these complex dives.

It always helps to watch a dive done correctly and then figure out what skills you need to learn. Tape a championship diving meet on TV and try to break down each part of a dive into its separate skills. Don't just look at what's going on in the air. Look at the approaches and hurdles, too.

Concentrate first on improving a specific part of the dive and it will be easier to combine the simple skills into a more complicated dive later. For example, let's say you want to learn a single back somersault in tuck position. When you first start to learn dives in the back dive group, your coach may ask you to simply jump backward off the 1-meter board to help you develop balance and learn how far you need to be from the board's edge for safety. Then you will learn a back dive tuck, which is really a half somersault. To help you progress to the full somersault in the tuck position, you may practice doing it in a belt with a competent spotter from a standing position on a gymnastics mat. Finally, you will combine the somersault with the correct back press from the board into a complete dive into the water.

Again, safety is the primary reason coaches teach skill progressions. Each dive starts with slightly different core skills. Your coach can explain the order of each skill to best learn a particular dive. The more you dive, the easier it will be to know which skills you need to improve on, before moving through lead-up to complex dives.

Fine-tuning Your Water Entry Skills

Some practices may consist of working on your vertical entries, or *line-ups*. One way coaches teach line-ups is by having you stand or sit on the edge of a springboard or platform. The arm and body positions vary, depending on which dive group or dive you're practicing.

Drop off the board or platform into a completely extended line-up with hands together, arms over your head, keeping your hips and knees straight. As your line-ups improve, gradually you will learn to rip your entries.

Coaches also teach divers how to avoid belly flops and near misses by playing the "Dive or Jump Game." After take-off, your coach yells out "Dive!" or "Jump!" You must react quickly to line up your body head first if you hear "dive" or feet first if you hear "jump." This teaches you to make mid-air corrections and move into the correct position for a safe landing. The Dive or Jump Game helps you respond quickly to decide which way is up and which way is down.

You may also hear the term, *saving a dive*. A save is a movement you do underwater while you're entering to make it appear that you're vertical. In general, once you're under the water you continue to turn in the direction of your rotation above the water. A save helps the feet enter the water at the same place that the hands entered, giving spectators the illusion of a vertical entry.

Chapter 4

DIVING—READY FOR THE SCORES

*C*ompeting in a diving meet can be a challenging and thrilling experience. This is when you use all of your training and all of the knowledge you have learned in practice. You are competing, but you are also performing. You're out on the board all alone, like a dancer or a gymnast doing a solo performance in front of an audience.

All diving competitions are basically the same, whether it's a dual meet or a championship meet. For now, let's look at what happens during the diving portion of a summer league dual meet like the one described in Chapter 2 for swimming.

Age Group Diving Competitions

It's a Wednesday evening in July, and your team, the Red Tornadoes, is competing against your closest rival from across town, the Blue Devils. The meet is being held at the Blue Devils' outdoor pool, which is 12 feet deep in the diving end. The Blue Devils have both a 1-meter and a 3-meter springboard, but dual meets in your town's summer age group league use the 1-meter board only.

Your coach has asked you to be at the pool by 5:00 to warm up and to turn in the sheet of paper listing the dives you will be doing during the meet. This is your *dive list*.

The dive list also asks for your name and age group. The local divisions for springboard competition in some summer leagues and in many U.S. Diving age group competitions are 9-and-under, 10-11, 12-13, 14-15, 16-17 and 18-19. Some summer leagues may have only two age categories, the *Junior* division for divers 13 and under and the *Senior* division for divers 14-17.

Your league uses the 9-and-under, 10-11, 12-13, 14-15,

A back one and a half somersault dive in the straight position. The diver has just come out of the somersault. He will straighten his back, and move his arms over his head before entering the water.

16-17 and 18-19 age groups. Each team can enter one boy diver and one girl diver in each age group.

During the competition, each diver will do *required dives* and *optional dives*. The 9-and-unders and 10-11s will do two required dives and two optionals. The other age groups will do three required dives and two optionals.

We'll look at the difference between required dives and optional dives in a moment.

What the Judges Look For

There will be three meet judges—your diving coach, the Red Tornadoes' diving coach, and the swimming meet starter. They will score each dive from zero to 10 points. They can also give half points. Here is the standard scoring method used by U.S. Diving:

Very Good .... 8½ to 10 points
Good .... 6½ to 8 points
Satisfactory .... 5 to 6 points
Deficient .... 2½ to 4½ points
Unsatisfactory .... ½ to 2 points
Completely failed................ 0 points

After a dive, the judges each flash cards showing their scores for the dive. They do not discuss their scores with each other before showing their cards to the crowd. Also, they do not talk to each other about the dives during the competition. This helps make sure that the scoring is as fair as possible.

In deciding on a score for each dive, the judges look at the approach, the take-off, the position and grace of the body in the air, and the entry into the water. The judges are not supposed to consider how you got up onto the board or what you do under the water after you've dived into it.

Judges look to see that you are confident and relaxed, that you get into position in the air correctly, that your toes are pointed, and that you are fully extended for a straight up and down entry into the water.

The judges won't score you by comparing your dive to another diver's. They score you by comparing it to the way the dive should look if it were a perfect dive, or a "10."

With her legs straight, toes pointed and knees close to her chest, this diver shows perfect form in the pike position.

Required Dives, Optional Dives, and Degree of Difficulty

The required dives and optional dives you do are selected from the FINA Diving Table, which is the list of all dives used by U.S. Diving. Dives are grouped according to forward dives, back dives, reverse dives, inward dives, twisting dives and armstand dives. In front of each dive there is a number such as 101, 102, or 202 or 5121. This is called the *dive number.*

Each position is listed on the table according to the springboard or platform you will be using in the contest. The straight position is always in column A, pike position in column B, tuck position in column C, and free position in column D.

Finally, the number listed under each of the columns is the *degree of difficulty.* The degree of difficulty is used in figuring out the final score for each person's dive.

On your dive list, you must list the dive numbers and letters which match the descriptions of the dives you will do. You also list the degree of difficulty of each dive. The announcer will use this list to describe to the judges, the scorers and the crowd which dive is next.

Required dives are the basic dives everyone must know how to do before they master more complicated dives. Judges want to see that you can do basic dives with the same grace and athletic ability as fancy dives.

The required dives to choose from for the 9-and-unders and 10-11s on the 1-meter board are forward, back, reverse and inward dives in the tuck position (101C, 201C, 301C and 401C). For the older age groups the required dives also include dives in pike position and some twisting

An aerial view of a back dive in the open pike position.

dives. Optional dives include forward 1½ somersaults in pike and tuck positions (103B and C), back full somersault dives in pike and tuck positions (202B and C), reverse 1½ somersaults in pike or tuck (302B and C), and forward 1½ somersaults with a full twist in free position (5132D). Again, older divers have more optional dives from which to choose.

In the optional dives, you can cut loose and show off. These dives are complicated and require more position sense to know up from down. For this reason, they have higher degrees of difficulty. As you get older, you will have to add more and more optional dives to your list.

The degree of difficulty of each dive can make a big difference in the outcome of the competition. Here's why: The judges give their scores after each dive. When there are three judges, the scores are added together and the sum is then multiplied by the degree of difficulty. This gives you total points for your dive.

If the scores are 5, 4½, and 5½, the total is 15. If the degree of difficulty for the dive is 2.0, you multiply 15 times 2.0 and the final award for the dive is 30 points. You then add all of each diver's points to get each diver's total points for the meet. The diver with the highest total points wins the contest.

The degree of difficulty for younger age groups is sometimes changed. That will be the case at this dual meet for the 9-and-unders, the 10-11s and the 12-13s. For the 9-and-unders and 10-11s, *all* dives will have a degree of difficulty of 1.0. For the 12-13s, the required dives will have degrees of difficulty of 1.9 and the optional dives will have the degrees of difficulty listed in the FINA diving table.

Why are the degrees of difficulty sometimes changed? The degree of difficulty can make a difference in who wins the contest. There is a certain amount of strategy involved in picking and choosing which required and optional dives to do. For instance, let's say you have your choice of two dives. One is a dive with a low degree of difficulty, but you can perform it exceptionally well and score a lot of points. The other has a high degree of difficulty, but you have a hard time doing it well and don't score very high. But once the degree of difficulty of each dive is multiplied by your total points, you might end up getting more points on the difficult dive, even though you scored lower on the judges' scorecards.

Let's say that you've filled out your dive list now, and the two required dives you will do are a forward dive in the pike position and a back dive in the tuck position. Your two optional dives are an inward dive in the pike position and a forward 1½ somersault dive in the tuck position.

The swimmers will be through warming up at 5:30. That's when the divers start practicing.

You've never been on this board before, so you have to practice your approach several times to figure out where to start. You want to be able to land on the tip of the board after your hurdle.

The Competition Begins

Usually, one age group dives at a time and finishes the list before the next age group starts. Tonight, the youngest girl diver from your team will go first, and then the youngest girl diver from the Blue Devils team. Then the youngest boy diver from your team will go, followed by the youngest boy Blue Devil. You will have about two minutes to wait between each of your dives.

Your diving coach reminds you to relax and think about how you felt when you did well in practice the other day.

You know that you've been having a problem entering the water perfectly straight on your inward dive—you've been over-rotating slightly. But since that's your third dive

115

A back somersault in the tuck position. A somersault is one full rotation of your body either forward or backward, and can be done in any of the basic positions.

today, you're concentrating right now on your first dive, the forward dive in the pike position.

When it's your turn, you climb onto the board and change the fulcrum right after the diver before you enters the water. Do this while the judges are giving the scores for that diver. This way you'll be ready to stand relaxed, confident, and with proper body alignment while the announcer calls your name and the dive you're going to do.

"Dive 101-B, a forward dive in pike position, degree of difficulty one point zero."

Relax a second or two in your starting position. Once you begin, you must keep going. If you "start over," the dive will be declared a *balk*. If you begin your approach and then stop, the meet referee will instruct the announcer to reduce each judge's score by two points. If a diver balks twice on the same dive, it is considered a failed dive and no points are awarded.

But you're not having any problem with that today. In fact, you feel pretty good, so off you go! You do your approach and hurdle well and land right on the end of the board correctly. You could have pointed your toes a little more during your hurdle, and you could have gotten into a tighter pike position. Your entry is good but your feet come apart.

Even though your coach is judging, you can get some brief pointers between dives, and as you're coming out of the water. Your coach mentions the tighter pike and your feet coming apart. These aren't things that you did wrong. They're simply things to work on to improve the dive for later meets.

Now that your first dive is out of the way, it's time to think about your second required dive, the back dive in tuck position. Try to picture yourself getting a well-balanced back press so that you get high into the air before you tuck. Then picture yourself kicking your legs out straight before stretching as you sight the water for your entry.

It's always a good idea to rehearse in your mind. Focus on your next dive and it will help you stay relaxed and ready when the diver in front of you is going off the board.

When you finish your back dive, you know that your entry wasn't lined up straight. Now you are standing on the board for the third time while the announcer calls your inward dive in pike position. Instead of over-rotating, you are cautious this time. As a result, your line-up was far too "short" and you entered the water at an angle away from the board. You know you did it better in practice last week and think, "Why couldn't I do it the same way again?" But then you remind yourself you've got one more dive to concentrate on, so you put the inward dive out of your mind.

Your final dive, the forward 1½ somersaulting dive in the tuck position, is your favorite dive. You really like spinning in the air, and you always seem to line up the dive straight into the water. This time is no exception. You do a good job, and then that's it—your part of the diving competition is over. Now you can watch the rest of the divers and clap as they finish.

Sometimes the results are announced right after the last diver has finished. Tonight the meet is running late so they're going to get right back to the swimming and announce the diving results after the next event is over.

In the meantime, your coach reviews the good parts of your dives with you and discusses things to work on in upcoming practices. Your toe point in the air is really improving—you're getting to where you do it without having to think about it. You're also extending your body much more as you take off from the board.

Your coach also suggests you practice both tuck and pike positions on your inward dive while you work on improving your entry. It's good that you're trying the pike

The closed pike position. The diver's hands reach and grab behind her legs, slightly below the backs of her knees.

position, which is a harder dive, but you might learn more control practicing the tuck position as well. If you're able to master more skills this way, it could mean more points, since all the degrees of difficulty in your age group are the same.

It turns out that the other diver won, but you made such an improvement over the last time you dived that it doesn't seem to matter. Your friends on the team noticed too. Some of them have even come over to say, "Way to go!" So all in all, you feel pretty pleased. With more practice, you know you'll do even better next time.

Invitational Diving Meets

Dual meets that have both diving and swimming events can be exciting places to start diving competitively. However, not every city, town or county has a summer league program that competes in dual meets. You may begin training with a diving team that attends regional invitational meets, which are open to all divers living within a certain area. Invitational meets include many divers in each age group, and usually you have longer waits between your dives than you do at a dual meet.

Many invitational meets will have 3-meter springboard events. There may be a 5-meter platform event for 11-and-unders, and a 5-meter and 7.5-meter platform event for 12-13s. Ten-meter tower events may be held for divers ages 14 and up.

In many meets, there are *preliminaries* and *finals.* Sometimes if there is a large number of contestants, there is a "cut" after the preliminary dives to limit the number of divers who advance to the finals. During a morning session, you may compete in the preliminaries (*prelims*). If you finish in the top 8 or top 12 in your age group, you will advance to the finals, which will be held either later that day or on the next day. In the finals, the person who had the lowest score from the prelims goes first, and the person with the highest score will dive last.

If there are only five divers entered in your age group, you may still have to dive a prelim round to establish the diving order for the final round. A final round could include three or four optional dives that you didn't do in the prelims, or you may repeat the dives you did earlier.

It's fun to participate in invitationals because you get to meet and compete against people from other parts of the country. You can watch other divers and their coaches to get an idea of what they might be doing differently, and how they train. It can also be nice to compete as a team where diving is the only aquatic sport involved.

Willingness to Perform

All of the physical skills for moving your body gracefully and skillfully through the air can be further helped by simply being eager and willing to demonstrate the

A reverse dive, just after the diver has completed her hurdle and take off and reversed direction in mid-air. A reverse dive is the most difficult of the four basic dive groups.

skills in front of other people. This is sometimes called a *willingness to perform.* A willingness to perform can help you in practice when you try to make the corrections your coach recommends, but it is particularly helpful during competition.

Diving in competition is more stressful to some kids than to others. It's like stage fright for an actor. The actor may have rehearsed the part a hundred times and then suddenly, out of nervousness, forget the lines right before going onstage. With experience, though, actors learn to relax and trust that they can repeat in front of an audience exactly what they've rehearsed. In fact, there's something about the energy the crowd generates that can help the actor perform better than she did during rehearsal.

The same holds true in diving. In practices, you've taught your body how to move during the dives you will be using in competition. Relax between dives at a meet and concentrate on doing one dive at a time. You can't fail if you enjoy the good dives and resolve to improve the ones you can do better.

Every actor flubs a line some time, but an actor can't walk off the stage and bring the play to a stop. The actor must recover and keep going. Divers go through the same thing. It's not a disaster to occasionally do a dive poorly, or even blow a dive. It's an opportunity to learn and do better on your next dive.

A good example is Cynthia Potter, who won 28 national titles during her diving career. Cynthia once completely slipped off the board on a back dive at the National Championships. She did manage to land head first in the water so the judges could not award zeroes. She received scores of ½ point from each judge, which kept her in the contest.

At the first cut, she was in 16th place and was the last diver to advance. She kept doing great dives after her disastrous back dive and finished 8th in the prelims, making her the last diver to advance to the finals. Then, in the finals, she went on to win!

Additional Resources

If you want to learn as much as possible about diving in a short period of time, a summer diving camp could be educational and a lot of fun. You'll not only get new coaching tips, you'll meet people interested in diving who could become good friends. Each diving camp is set up a little bit differently depending upon who is coaching it, what the available training facilities are, which skill levels will be taught, and how many days it will last. Your coach and parents can help you decide which camp would be a good one to attend. Magazines such as *Swimming World* and *Rip* list summer diving camps in their spring issues.

United States Diving also has several books you can purchase that can help you learn more about diving training and diving safety. You can also purchase the current U.S. Diving Rules and Regulations through the U.S. Diving office. Contact them at the address below for current prices and availability of their source materials and referrals for competitive diving programs in your area:

United States Diving, Inc.
Pan American Plaza
201 S. Capital Ave., Suite 430
Indianapolis, IN 46225

GLOSSARY

SWIMMING

Aerobic: With oxygen. When the intake of oxygen equals the use of oxygen within the muscles. Distance swimming events are more aerobic than sprinting events.

Anaerobic: Without oxygen. When muscles require more oxygen than the body is able to take in during the specific exercise. Diving and sprinting events in swimming are anaerobic.

Backstroke Flags: Ropes with colored plastic triangles hung over each end of the pool. When backstrokers see these flags, they know they're getting close to the wall. In 50-meter pools, backstroke flags are 5 meters from each end. In 25-meter and 25-yard pools, the flags are 15 feet (or 4.57 meters) from each end.

Bulkhead: The wall or platform that divides a pool into different courses, such as a 50-meter pool into the 25-yard courses.

Circle Swimming: Swimmers stay to the right of the black line during workout to enable more swimmers to train in each lane.

Counters: Plastic cards with numbers on them used to keep track of laps during distance freestyle races of 400 yards or more.

Distance per Stroke: How far you swim with each arm pull.

DQ: Disqualify, or disqualification. Also, *DQ'd* for disqualified. Referees disqualify swimmers for breaking stroke rules or for making false starts.

Drag: The resistance water gives to your body as you swim.

Drag Suit: The second loose-fitting swimsuit you wear during workout or warm-up to add weight and resistance.

Drill: An exercise designed to improve one specific part of a swimmer's stroke.

Dry Land Training: Any exercises swimmers do out of the water to help them swim faster.

Entry Form: A form you fill out to enter a swim meet. It usually requires your name, age, sex, event, seed time, and U.S. Swimming Registration Number.

False Start: If the starter says "take your mark" and then a swimmer moves on the block or jumps into the water before the gun or horn sounds, the swimmer is charged with a false start. A false start in a relay happens when a swimmer's feet leave the block before the swimmer coming in to the wall touches.

Flip Turn: A turn in freestyle or backstroke where the swimmer tumbles and changes direction with the head under water.

Glide: When your body continues to move in the water after finishing an arm pull, leg kick, a push off the wall, or a dive.

Gutter: The edge of the pool where water overflows before being circulated back into the pool.

Heats & Finals: A type of meet where you compete in the heats of an event to qualify among the top six or eight swimmers. These fastest swimmers race the event again in the final heat to determine the final placings.

Interval: How much time you have to finish a repeat before you start again.

Kickboard: A plastic or styrofoam board used to isolate your legs during kicking drills.

Lap Gun: In distance freestyle events longer than 400 yards, the meet starter fires the lap gun when the leader of a race has only two more laps to finish. At some competitions, a bell might be used instead of the gun.

Legal: A race or stroke swum according to current USS rules and regulations.

Log Book: A book swimmers sometimes use to list workouts swum and times achieved at meets.

Long Course: A 50-meter pool.

Negative Split: Swimming the last half of a race faster than the front half.

Official: One of the judges at a meet who makes sure swimmers are competing according to USS rules. Officials include the start, stroke and turn judges, and timers.

Open Turn: A turn made at the end of the pool where the swimmer's head is kept out of the water.

Pace Clock: Large clock with a big second hand and smaller minute hand that swimmers use to start interval or repeat drills. The numbers around the face of the clock are in seconds (5, 10, 15, etc.) rather than in hours (1, 2, 3, etc.), with the number 60 at the top.

Pull Buoy: Pieces of styrofoam you hold between your legs to isolate the arms during pulling drills.

Qualifying Time (Cut Time): Some meets have qualifying or cut times listed for each event. You have to either equal or swim faster than the cut time before the entry deadline for the meet in order to swim the event.

Repeat: Each of the individual distances you swim during an interval set. An example is 10 x 50 freestyles on 1:30. Each 50 freestyle is a repeat, for a total of 10. Each repeat is started every one and a half minutes.

Scratch: To withdraw from a race.

Seeding: The way meet officials organize all the swimmers entered in an event into one or more heats. Seeding can be either fastest-to-slowest or slowest-to-fastest.

Set: The name for a whole group of repeat swims. You might do a set of *5 x 100 I.M.* or a set of *10 x 25 freestyle.*

Short Course: A 25-meter pool or a 25-yard pool.

Split: If you split a race or workout distance into segments, the time for each segment is the split time, or "split" for short.

Sprint: "A sprint" can be the name of a stroke event 100 yards or meters or less. "To sprint" means to swim as fast as possible over a short distance.

Streamline: The position you want to take to make your body as straight and smooth as possible. Being streamlined keeps drag in the water to a minimum.

Stroke: Either one arm pull, or one of the four types of swimming styles (backstroke, butterfly, breaststroke and freestyle).

Swim-Off: Sometimes more than one swimmer does the same qualifying time during heats and it results in too many swimmers for the number of lanes available in the final. To determine which of the tied swimmers gets to move on to the final, the same race event will be swum again. This extra race is a swim-off.

Taper: The days of training before a big meet when your coach gives you more rest during workouts.

Timed Finals: These are the heats in a meet where you swim each race only once to determine the final placings.

Touch Pad: The pad at the end of each lane where a swimmer's time is recorded and sent electronically to the timing system and scoreboard.

USS: United States Swimming, Inc. The national governing body for amateur competitive swimming in America.

Warm-Down: The laps you do after a race to help your body recover to normal (sometimes called the "cool-down").

Warm-Up: The laps you do at the beginning of a workout or before a race to get the muscles loose and ready to swim your best.

Diving

Alignment: When your head, shoulders, hips and legs are held in a straight line.

Approach: From your starting position, the approach is the number of steps you take to the end of the board on forward and reverse dives, before the hurdle.

Armstand Dive: A dive that starts from the edge of a platform in an armstand (or handstand).

Back Dive: Back dives start with the diver balancing on the balls of her feet facing away from the water.

Balk: An illegal movement by a diver: (1) a false start after assuming the starting position, where the diver clearly starts but doesn't complete the dive; (2) Jumping from 2 feet rather than 1 foot to start the hurdle; (3) When the diver's feet touch the platform by losing balance at the start of an armstand dive.

Center of Gravity: The point in a diver's body around which a diver twists or tumbles.

Cut-Through Dive: A type of armstand dive where the diver's legs swing down toward the platform after take off.

Degree of Difficulty: (D.D.) A rating for each dive that ranks how hard it is to perform. D.D.'s range from 1.0 to 3.5, and they're multiplied by the judges' scores to determine a diver's total points for a dive.

Dive List: The group of dives you will perform in a meet. You list the dives on a form that you hand to an official before the meet starts.

Draw: The order the divers will perform in a meet. Names printed on pieces of paper are usually shuffled and drawn by chance one at a time.

Entry: When the diver goes into the water. On most dives the entry is head first, but full somersaulting dives are feet first.

Finalist: A diver who competes in an event's finals.

Finals: The contest that determines the final placings of each diver.

Flat-hand Entry: Grabbing your hands together or spreading them into a flat blunt shape to "punch a hole" in the water. This creates little splash and helps you rip it.

Flight: The path of the dive in the air.

Forward Dive: A dive that begins facing the water where you rotate away from the board through the air.

Fulcrum: A wheel that rolls under the middle of the springboard that you move to give the board more bounce or less bounce.

Free Position: Used in twisting dives only, the free position is any combination of straight, pike or tuck positions that helps you finish a dive.

Hang Time: The extra time you have in the air before you begin your descent, achieved by a strong, high take-off.

Hurdle: The jump from one foot you take at the end of the approach on a forward or reverse dive, to the two-foot landing on the end of the board before the take-off.

Inward Dive: Starts the same as a back dive, but once in the air the diver rotates in a direction toward the board.

Kick-out: The sudden knee and hip extension you make after finishing a somersault that helps you slow your rotation to line up your body vertically for entry.

Lead-up: A specific skill that helps you do a more complicated move later.

Line Up: A vertical entry into the water with straight, extended body alignment.

Pike Position: When the body is bent at the hips but with knees still straight.

Platform: The levels on a diving tower. Platforms are 1, 3, 5, 7.5 and 10 meters high.

Plummet Line: An imaginary line from the tip of a board or diving platform straight down to the water surface.

Preliminaries: A group of dives by competitors at a meet that determines who qualifies for the finals. Sometimes called "prelims" for short.

Press: The press is the drop of the heels and body into the squat position.

Referee: An official who makes sure all diving rules and regulations are being observed. The referee is not a judge.

Reverse Dive: A dive that starts like a forward dive, but once you're in the air you change positions so that you rotate backward towards the board.

"Riding the Board": When you get the maximum height possible from the board.

Rip Entry: A type of competitive diving entry with little or no splash that sounds like a piece of paper being ripped.

Save: After something about the dive goes wrong "saving a dive" means recovering to finish as vertically as possible.

Skill Progressions: A series of skills you learn ranging from easy to hard.

Somersault: When your body moves head over heels on the ground or in the air. Intervals of rotation are ½, full, 1½, 2, etc.

Spot: A place to look at during a somersaulting dive to be sure you're going straight up and down for the entry. On a 2½ somersaulting dive, you see your spot twice.

Spotter: A person who assists to make sure an exercise is being performed safely.

Springboard: The 16-foot flexible bouncing board approved for 1-meter and 3-meter competitions.

Straight Position: When the body is in alignment with no bends at the knees or hips. Also called "layout" position.

Take-off: The time on the board from final depression and recoil to last contact preceding flight.

Photo Credits

Mike Hastings/The Diver: 81, 89, 109
Mary Messenger: 18
Al Messerschmidt: 10, 12, 30, 53, 83, 111, 113, 116, 119, 121, 123
Rich Clarkson/Sports Illustrated: 17, 54, 69
Manny Millan/Sports Illustrated: 24, 58, 64, 106
Ronald C. Modra/Sports Illustrated: 6, 14, 75, 78, 86, 97, 99
Tony Tomsic/Sports Illustrated: 8, 60, 71